John George Mac Carthy

A Plea for the Home Government of Ireland

John George Mac Carthy

A Plea for the Home Government of Ireland

ISBN/EAN: 9783744713887

Printed in Europe, USA, Canada, Australia, Japan

Cover: Foto ©ninafisch / pixelio.de

More available books at **www.hansebooks.com**

FOR THE

HOME GOVERNMENT

OF

IRELAND.

BY

JOHN GEORGE MACCARTHY,

AUTHOR OF

' IRISH LAND QUESTIONS PLAINLY STATED AND ANSWERED
ETC.

LONDON:
LONGMANS, GREEN, AND CO.
1871.

CONTENTS.

A PLEA

FOR THE

HOME GOVERNMENT

OF

IRELAND.

———•◦•———

CHAPTER I.

Prefatory.

THE proposal to let the local affairs of Ireland be administered by an Irish Representative Assembly has now 'come to the front' for public discussion and parliamentary settlement. As usually happens with new or newly-revived political proposals, it is the subject of all sorts of misconceptions. Hence it may be of some use to state shortly what the proposal is, why it is considered reasonable, what practical advantages are expected from it, and what answers are suggested to the objections raised against it.

B

This has been done already by Mr. BUTT, M.P., and others, with an ability and authority which I do not possess.*   But, however the proposal be disposed of, it is an important one, and ought to be considered from many points of view.   Candid and impartial enquirers may like to know how it looks from the point of view of a professional man living in an Irish provincial city, minding his own business, having no quarrel with anybody in Ireland or out of it, and whose only interest in the matter is, that whatever is really best for all concerned should be done.

'Tall' talk may, I think, be advantageously omitted from both sides of the discussion. It is natural and excusable that Irishmen should sometimes write angrily about England, and that Englishmen should sometimes write scornfully about Ireland.   But anger

---

* See Mr. BUTT's statesmanlike brochure on *Irish Federalism*, of which three editions have been published by Mr. Falconer, of Dublin; the remarkably able and thoughtful series of articles from the pen of Mr. MAGUIRE, M.P., which appeared in the *Cork Examiner*, and are now in course of republication; also the eloquent and learned addresses made to the Dublin Corporation, by Messrs. O'NEILL DAUNT, MARTIN, M.P., and Professor GALBRAITH, republished by the Home Government Association.

and scorn, however natural and excusable, are not conducive to the useful discussion of weighty matters, to the clear statement of one's views, or to the fair appreciation of the views and arguments of others. Besides, it may be hoped that the time for anger and scorn between reasonable Englishmen and Irishmen has passed. 'Byegones' may now be 'byegones.' No fair-minded Irishman can fail to be touched by the generous efforts which Mr. GLADSTONE and most Englishmen worth counting have recently made to find out what is best for Ireland and to do it. No fair-minded Englishman can fail to see the unreasonableness of expecting other people to think precisely as he does, and denouncing anybody who differs as a knave or a fool. 'Centuries of not always ill-intentioned mistakes' may be, and ought to be, forgiven by the nation that has suffered them ; but they should, at least, leave behind them a lesson of caution to the nation that has committed them. I trust it is not offensive to suggest that those who have admittedly made a series of disastrous blunders in the past ought not to be

overweeningly confident in dealing with the
present or the future.

I see clearly that with most Englishmen it
needs an effort to consider this question at
all. The very raising it is considered an
impertinence, almost a treason. The staunch-
est friends of Ireland view it with alarm,
contempt, and indignation. They say, in
effect; 'We have gone with you very far;
we have sacrificed for you our own predilec-
tions and given up our own ways; we have
let our most urgent political and social business wait in order to attend to yours; we
have tried with all our strength to do you
justice at last; we will do still more for you
if you will only let us : but this proposal of
Home Government for Ireland is utterly unreasonable. It is childish; it is dangerous; it is
"wild;" it is ungrateful; it is bad for yourselves,
is bad for us; it is Fenianism, Communism,
Ultramontanism. We cannot even discuss it;
our only answer to it is; "No!"' For this
state of feeling I have a real deference. Men
and journals speak and write thus who by
their past services to us have earned the right

to speak and write bluntly. It is quite pro-
bable that if I occupied their point of view,
I would be disposed to think and write in
the same strain. But, however so disposed I
might be, I am quite certain I would do that
which I now respectfully ask every fair-minded
English reader of these pages to do, namely,
to put aside all such preconceptions as much
as possible, to shake off the trammels of
routine, and to consider the question on its
merits, without passion and without prejudice.
It is not generally considered wise, or even
dignified, to refuse to hear argument. 'Stat
pro ratione voluntas' is not ordinarily deemed
to be a maxim of true statesmanship or of
sound political philosophy. James II. was
fond of declaring that he would not discuss;
but the result was not satisfactory from his
point of view.

After all, nearly every great reform, when
first proposed, was considered repulsive, chi-
merical, almost treasonable, and was declared
by many eminent persons to be quite outside
the pale of discussion. Catholic Emancipation, Municipal Reform, Free Trade, the

Church Disestablishment, the Land-law Reform : each of these was at first deemed to be the 'crotchet' of a few foolish or dangerous men, and the cloak of some ruinous 'ism ;' was denounced by Parliament, by the press, and by the country for years ; but being, in the main, right, and being, in the main, honestly promoted, got on as we know ; came to be eloquently advocated from the very ministerial benches whence it had been indignantly denounced or mercilessly 'chaffed ;' came to be ably pleaded for in the very journals that at first refused even to discuss it ; was voted by great majorities, and with tumultuous cheers, in the very Legislature where it had long been considered almost a jest : until at length the 'crotchet' of the few became, with the assent of most reasonable people, the law of the land, and what was once looked on as dangerous to social order, was found to be a true safe-guard to the State.   It would be rash to predict that the Home Rule proposal will run the same course.   But it would be not less rash to reject without enquiry any political proposal

on the sole ground of its being at variance
with preconceived ideas. The true friend of
social order is he who finds out and tries to
advance what is really best for society, whether it be novel or accustomed, vulgar or
fashionable.

It is to fellow-Irishmen, however, this plea
is chiefly addressed. I suppose if we, Irishmen, all agreed on the desirableness of the
proposed change it would soon be made.
But, as usual, we are very far indeed from
being agreed. A few able, thoughtful, and
distinguished men of various creeds, classes,
and parties, have made the proposal. It
has had considerable influence. It has made
some way at the hustings : it seems likely
to make much more way. It has made
still more important way in the minds of
quiet non-political people all over the country.
Calm, sensible, clear-headed men are inclining
towards it from all sides, all ranks, and all
creeds. Most of the leading Irish journals
have declared for it. So have the principal
Irish municipal bodies. It has moved the
popular mind more than any political pro-

posal for a quarter of a century. Nevertheless, the most eminent, the most representative, and the most distinguished Irishmen of all classes still reserve their adhesion to it. I honour their prudent and manly reserve. Ireland would, indeed, be unfit to manage its own affairs if its leading men did not examine so important a proposal with the very keenest scrutiny and the very coolest circumspection. Nothing is more personally cowardly, nothing is more nationally perilous, than the surrender of real opinions to the ever-shifting requirements of popular feeling. In public affairs, as in private, there is often real virtue and real courage in saying 'No.' I do not ask any man to say 'Yes' to this proposal until he has given it the fullest consideration, and unless he be convinced, after reviewing the whole matter as a shrewd and sensible man would view a matter of importance in his own private affairs, that it is really desirable for all concerned. I venture to hope that the following pages may suggest something in favour of such a conclusion.

CHAPTER II.

The Proposal.

THE Proposal in question, as authoritatively stated by the HOME GOVERNMENT ASSOCIATION, is, in effect, this : that the internal affairs of Ireland be regulated by an Irish Parliament, consisting of the Queen, Lords, and Commons of Ireland : all Imperial affairs, and all that relates to the Colonies, Foreign States, and the common interests of the Empire continuing to be regulated by the Imperial Parliament, in which (but only on Imperial questions) Ireland would continue to be represented.

The idea at the bottom of this proposal is the desirableness of finding some safe middle course between separation on the one hand, and over-centralization on the other. It is clearly undesirable to separate politically two countries which are so nearly associated geographically, so closely connected socially, with so many common interests commercially and internationally. It is no less clearly undesirable that one country should virtually control the domestic affairs of another country, whose genius, likings, and dislikings it, confessedly, does not understand, to whose business it, admittedly, has not time to attend, and whose national life the very existence of such domestic control necessarily stunts and emasculates. The HOME GOVERNMENT ASSOCIATION says in effect : Here is a statesmanlike middle-course, a wise adaptation of constitutional principles to actual facts. Let there be a division of legislative and executive labour. Let an Irish Assembly manage exclusively Irish affairs : let the Imperial Parliament continue to manage all that relates to the Empire at large. Retain every guarantee for the real and effective unity of the Empire ; but let Great Britain and Ireland each transact its own private business as each deems best. Let both neighbours combine for every neighbourly purpose, and pull together, if need be, against the rest of the world as good neighbours should ; but let each give up, once

for all, the arrogant and mischievous pretension of lording it over the hearthstone and
dictating the domestic economy of the other.
Thus will be combined National freedom with
Imperial strength.

Such is the proposal in question : and
such is its ' idée mère.'

Its details must necessarily be matters of
subsequent adjustment. In the order of every
well-regulated discussion the principle comes
first, the details afterwards. If the principle
were once adopted the details would come
to be settled between the best heads of all
parties in both countries. There ought not
to be much real difficulty in settling them.
Precedents abound in history and in the
actual life of many of the greatest of existing
communities. A good precedent was put on
our own statute book only four years ago
(30 Vic., C. III.) Eminent statesmen and
great jurists of various ages and nations have
thought over every point long ago. Still it
is reasonable that some advocate of the
present proposal should sketch out some such
details. This has been well done by Mr.

BUTT, M.P., himself a jurist of eminent rank.* The HOME GOVERNMENT ASSOCIATION, while declining to pledge itself to details, has formally sanctioned Mr. BUTT'S suggestions. The following is a summary of them:—

As to the Crown : it is not proposed to affect its prerogatives at all. The only change would be that in exclusively Irish matters it would be guided by the advice of an Irish Parliament, and an Irish Ministry. In all other affairs it would continue, as at present, to be guided by the advice of the Imperial Legislature.

As to the Imperial Parliament : it would continue to have precisely the same supreme powers that it now possesses over all Imperial affairs : just as completely as if no Irish Parliament existed. Its jurisdiction would include every international transaction; all relations with foreign states : all questions of peace and war : the government of the colonies : the army, navy, and all that relates to the defence and stability of the Empire : control of the Imperial customs and general

* *Irish Federalism.* Dublin : Falconer. 3rd Ed.

trade regulations : control of expenditure and supplies for all Imperial purposes : power to levy general taxation for such purposes : charge of the public debt and the Imperial Civil List : and sovereign power within the limits of its attributions over individual citizens of both countries. But it should be settled beforehand in what proportion Ireland should contribute to such expenditure : with what share of the public debt it is fairly chargeable : what part of the Imperial Civil List it should pay ; and taxation should be adjusted, not only as to amount but as to mode, in such a manner that its burden would be equitably distributed throughout every part in the United Kingdom. Of course, Ireland would continue to be represented in the Imperial Parliament on Imperial questions ; but on these only. For all Imperial purposes the two countries would continue to be an 'United Kingdom,' and to constitute in the face of other nations one Imperial State.

As to the Irish Parliament : it would have supreme control of the internal affairs of Ireland, just as if no Imperial Parliament existed.

Its jurisdiction would include every exclusively Irish interest: education, agriculture, commerce, manufactures, public works, courts of justice, magistracy, public railways, post office, corporations, grand juries, and every other detail of Irish business and Irish national life. If deemed desirable, however, it might be arranged that the establishment of any religious ascendancy, or the alteration of the Acts which settled Irish property in the reign of Charles II., should be placed beyond its jurisdiction. It would be composed of the Sovereign, Lords, and Commons of Ireland. The sovereignty of both Kingdoms would continue, and would be declared, to be indissolubly united. The House of Peers would consist of all Irish peers whose peerages date from before the Union (permanent absentees being omitted,) and such others as the Queen might call to the Upper Council of the Nation. The House of Commons might consist of representatives of the county constituencies, of the chief cities, of all towns with populations exceeding three thousand, of smaller towns grouped like the

Scotch burghs, of the universities, of the College of Physicians, &c., so as to effect a really popular representation, and at the same time secure to property and intelligence their just weight and influence. The franchise might be as at present. Voting would probably be best by ballot. In respect of all exclusively Irish interests the Irish Parliament, so constituted, would rank, act, and rule as the Parliament of an independent Nation.

But how prevent the clashing of these two co-ordinate jurisdictions? Mr. BUTT does not make any suggestion on this point. It would doubtless be a problem of difficulty and require grave ultimate consideration. It cannot, however, be impossible for the genius and statesmanship of both kingdoms to solve a problem that has been successfully solved in nearly every age of the world's history, and in nearly every region of civilized life. I suggest the solution that has worked so well elsewhere, namely : strict definitions of the limits of both jurisdictions, and a Supreme Court, independent of both, to interpret and maintain such definitions. Thus internal freedom and Imperial unity have, (with one memorable exception,) been reconciled in America ; and thus in Austro-Hungary the jurisdiction of the Hungarian Landtag has been adjusted with that of the Imperial Reichsrath.

Such, then, is the proposal, in principle and in detail.

We shall proceed to consider whether it be reasonable or unreasonable, advantageous or disadvantageous, and whether the balance of arguments be for or against it. But, before doing so, let us clear away some obvious errors from the path of discussion.

In the first place, I submit that it is obviously erroneous to suggest that the proposal is a vague or unintelligible one. It is perfectly clear and definite, and quite abundant in detail. Nothing more definite or detailed is possible—except the Bill embodying it for parliamentary discussion. This, I suppose, will be ready when the occasion arrives.

In the next place, I submit that it is obviously erroneous to describe the proposal as one for separation, or its advocates as Separatists. The preservation of the real and effective political unity of the Empire is one of its two primary and essential constituents. Whether it would really conduce to such unity, or be prejudicial to it, is a matter for discussion. But to say that it is a proposal for separation is, I submit, to commit an error, and to raise a false issue. No one calls the States of America (where the proposed system prevails,) separate States: they are, in fact, as in name, 'united;' and when separation was proposed, we know how vital the difference was considered. Federal union is one thing: separation is quite another thing: no good can come of confusing, in language or in thought, two things so absolutely different. It will facilitate useful discussion if this be kept in mind. I read every day able and eloquent arguments based on the supposition that this proposal is one for separation. Most of those arguments are not only able and eloquent, but true and useful. They are, however, as irrelevant to the proposal of the

HOME GOVERNMENT ASSOCIATION as if they were arguments about ENCKE's comet or the Darwinian theory.

Again : I submit that it is an obvious error to describe the proposal as communistic, or revolutionary. Of course angry and unscrupulous people will say whatever suits the temper or the convenience of the moment. With such disputants I have nothing to do ; I address only those who wish to be just, and to conduct a momentous controversy in a fair, cautious, and conciliatory spirit. These will readily admit that to apply such language to such a proposal is to abuse language. The proposal contains no one characteristic of communism. It violates no one principle of the constitution. It aims, (whether rightly or wrongly is to be seen,) at the constitutional prevention of over-centralization, that social malady apart from which communism is scarcely ever found.

But it is said that there is an ' arrière-pensée :' that this apparently reasonable and moderate proposal is but the cloak of some deep communistic design, the outwork beneath which traitors plot against the common weal. This objection, however, would reduce the debate from a discussion of principles to a discussion of persons. Moreover, it imposes on whoever raises it the obligation of justifying it. It is not a light thing to make such an accusation against known and responsible men, members of Parliament, grave ecclesiastics of both Churches, well known journalists, eminent lawyers, landed proprietors, leading merchants, and presidents of great commercial institutions. In common fairness, we must hold the accusation to be false until it is proved. For myself, I know it to be false and incapable of proof. It is not merely false : to any one who knows the men it is comically false. One cannot think of it without smiling. It reminds one of the famous discoveries that Mr. DISRAELI is chief of the Carbonari, and that Mr. GLADSTONE's object in life is a Cardinal's hat.

But it is said that the advocates of Home Rule are tools ; that nameless traitors lurk behind them ; that they are the unconscious instruments of a malign conspiracy whose

ends they do not know, and if they knew
would hate; that they are waifs of the great
flood of Democracy which is rising in all
lands and threatens to engulf all civilization.
To this I answer that it is impossible to
argue with vague apprehensions. In every
age of the world, in every social phase, in
every man's individual life, there are risks
and dangers to be encountered. These
dangers demand circumspection, prudence,
shrewdness, forethought. By all means
exercise such qualities in dealing with the
matter in hand. Provide against every real
danger. Scrutinise every actual circumstance.
But do not ask us to tremble before babyish
bogies, or shiver with the dread of unknown
evils. There is danger in dealing with a
moving steam-engine; but the most dangerous thing you can do respecting it is to sit
on the valve.

Lastly: I submit it is an obvious error to
refuse to consider a political proposal until all
its advocates are completely agreed on it,
and all its adherents express themselves
about it with the soundest statesmanlike

discretion and in the finest literary state. No political proposal would ever be ripe for discussion if these tests were necessary. PEEL would have refused to reform the corn laws until the Chartist leaders had become reconciled with the Whig Dukes. GLADSTONE would have refused religious equality until the ' levellers up ' had settled with the ' levellers down.' No one would ever have approached a settlement of the land question in face of the multifarious theories of 1869— theories which ranged from slight modifications of stamp duties to wholesale confiscation. The advocates of every proposal necessarily differ in character, in principle, in points of view, in matters of taste. All we can fairly ask is that which in the present case we have got, namely, a definite proposal from an authorised body.

CHAPTER III.

Is it Reasonable?

IN discussing any political proposal there are two things to be considered : first, its theoretical soundness, or, as people say, its reasonableness ; second, its practical advantages or disadvantages. In this chapter we shall consider the proposal in its theoretical aspect.

A political proposal may be said to be theoretically sound (1) when it is such as an impartial man of common sense would approve of for dealing with the facts of the case ; (2) when it is such as political philosophy prescribes for dealing with such a state of facts ; and (3) when it is such as historical experience shows works well in such a state of facts.

Let us apply these three tests to the present proposal.

I.

But, first, what are the facts ? They are so familiar to us that any statement of them must appear trite. Nevertheless, it will be far from waste of time to set them down here plainly and impartially as any intelligent stranger, (let me suppose the BABOO CHUNDER SEN, if I may be permitted this liberty with the distinguished gentleman's name,) might set them down in his note-book. Let us try to 'see oursels as others see us.'

Great Britain and Ireland (CHUNDER SEN might note) are two islands lying near each other in the Western Ocean. Both islands taken together constitute the home of a vast and famous Empire whose power is felt in all lands, and whose children have planted great colonies on every continent. They are separated from the rest of the world, at one side by 'a melancholy ocean,' at the other side by a 'streak of silver sea.' They are separated from each other by from thirty to a hundred miles of stormy water. The inhabitants of both islands, with few exceptions, speak the same language, read the same literature, and possess the same institutions. Ties of kinship, of friendship, and of association are innumerable between them. The commercial interests of both islands are nearly identical. Both are inhabited by the same races, but in different proportions : Celts predominating in Ireland, Saxons and Normans in Great Britain. Catholicity and Protestantism prevail in both, but in different proportions : in Ireland the former predominating, in Great Britain the latter. Great Britain is much larger and much more populous; but Ireland is larger than many independent kingdoms, and constitutes in itself a great, populous, and fruitful country. In many respects the Irish community is like that of the sister island : in many respects it is unlike. Historically, Ireland is the elder : it was a civilised and famous nation while England was a remote and barbarous Roman province. But English power, skill, and culture afterwards reversed the balance ; and for many centuries Great Britain has been rich, prosperous, and free, while Ireland has been poor, miserable, and subject. During these centuries England always asserted, more or less successfully, its domination : Ireland always struggled, more or less unsuccessfully, for its independence and individual life. RODERICK O'CONNOR, HUGH O'NEILL, OWEN ROE O'NEILL, SARSFIELD, EMMETT, and FITZGERALD, O'CONNELL and DAVIS, are all heroes of the same story. 1172, 1642, 1782, 1800, 1803, 1829, 1844, 1848 are all epochs of the same struggle. For six hundred years Ireland had a national legislative assembly, more or less free, of its own. About seventy years ago the influence of Great Britain, exerted in a manner and by expedients which all admit to be indefensible, abolished the Irish Assembly, and extinguished the individual existence of Ireland as a nation. Since then both islands have been ruled on the supposition that they were one homogeneous country, and Ireland ' West Britain.' From some cause this experiment of completely centralised rule has not proved satisfactory to either island. The two communities have not been fused into one : they do

not seem likely so to be fused. Ireland sends a
contingent of representatives to the Imperial
Parliament in London ; but this contingent
is necessarily divided in itself, and is practically outnumbered and overpowered by the
representatives of Great Britain.   The result
is that Great Britain virtually rules Ireland,
nominates her administrators, decides on
every detail of her internal life, and every law
of her social and political existence.   All that
the representatives of Irish national wishes
can do is to ' chaffer with successive minis-
tries, buying concessions at one time with
votes given at another time.'   At first Great
Britain ruled Ireland very badly indeed :
selfishly, ignorantly, and carelessly.   British
interests, real or supposed, British wishes,
reasonable or foolish, British laws, suitable or
unsuitable, were forced on the subject country.
Latterly, under Mr. GLADSTONE's generous
leadership, Great Britain has been trying hard
to rule Ireland well.   For this purpose it has
made great efforts, long studies, and some
sacrifices.   But, somehow, it does not ' hit it
off.'   Englishmen are continually declaring

that they 'cannot understand Ireland.'
Irishmen are continually complaining of
England. There are apparently unalterable
moral differences between the two countries.
What one likes the other dislikes. They are
scarcely ever in accord about anything.
Moreover, the Irish, however they may differ
amongst themselves, have many sympathies
in common : they generally glory in the
name of Ireland ; most of them are disposed
to grumble at having all effectual control of
their own domestic affairs taken from them,
and dislike to be governed by another community, whether it govern well or ill, whether
it be well-intentioned or ill-intentioned ;
some of them are every now and again
making efforts, occasionally wise, generally
foolish, to get the control of their own
affairs. The desire of national freedom and
the hope of it never left the national heart.
It occasionally rises to patriotism. It often
sinks into rowdyism. But it is nearly always
there—a vehement, deep-seated, wide-spread,
apparently indestructible national instinct,
underlying every agitation, outliving every

concession, flashing in the eye, flushing in
the cheek of most Irishmen and women, rich
and poor, educated and ignorant, Catholic and
Protestant, of Celtic descent and of Saxon
descent. Popular speakers know well, and
have known it any time these seventy years,
that if they want really to move any great
popular audience in Ireland, they can only
do so by striking this chord. Finally, the
British Parliament has got overwhelmed
with all sorts of work—English, Scotch,
Irish, Indian, American, Australian, political,
social, international, educational, financial,
commercial, military, naval, legal—insomuch
that it has arrived at a legislative ' choke ' or
' deadlock ; ' its members are overtaxed
almost beyond endurance ; the most urgent
Imperial business—business almost of life
and death to individuals and to the Empire
—has to be postponed for want of time to
attend to it ; and some division of legislative
labour appears to be indispensable if the public work is to be done at all, and both islands
saved from the disasters that inevitably
await neglect, confusion, and precipitancy.

Such is the state of things which both Englishmen and Irishmen have, for all our sakes, to look in the face, and which in fact is causing apprehension to prudent and thoughtful people in both countries.

Now, I submit, that any impartial and intelligent person (suppose the BABOO CHUNDER SEN,) if asked to suggest a remedy for this state of things, might reasonably suggest, as a matter of common sense and common business, the very proposal which the HOME GOVERNMENT ASSOCIATION have made. He might say in effect: discontinue this unsuccessful experiment of over-centralization, which is only a recent experiment at best: seek no further to treat as absolutely homogeneous two communities which are thus geographically, socially, and historically distinct; let there be a division of legislative labour; relieve the Imperial Parliament of the management of Irish internal affairs; let an Irish assembly look to these; let each country manage for itself what concerns itself only; let both manage in a common assembly what concerns both collectively. Thus healthy national aspirations will be satisfied; and the 'deadlock' of Imperial business prevented. Thus will a desirable mean be found between the separation of two countries which have so many interests in common, and the over-centralization which has been found to work so badly for both.

Surely, if the ' spectacles of routine ' be laid aside a little, and this proposal looked at impartially and naturally, it is not so very ' wild ' or far-fetched after all. I submit that it is, on the contrary, just what sound common sense would dictate for the advantage of all concerned, the welfare both of Ireland and Great Britain and the ultimate stability of the Empire.

II.

Common sense counts for a great deal ; but political philosophy, which ought to be the quintessence of common sense as applied to political affairs, counts for a great deal more. It is unwise to approach this question as if it were something new, as if the circumstances were unprecedented, or as if the way of dealing with such circumstances had never before been considered. I need scarcely remind any scholar that this question is nearly ' as old as the hills :' that the state of facts we have been considering is of frequent occurrence; and that the mode of dealing with it has engaged the heads of the best political thinkers from THALES to CALHOUN. From the earliest civilised times until now, and now in some of the greatest countries of the world, we find communities so united by circumstances of geographical position, of race, of commercial interests, and of civil institutions, that it is their interest to be joined in a common state, yet so distinct in internal structure, habitudes, and characteristics, or so separated by physical boundaries and national idiosyncracies, as to render it desirable that each should retain the management of its own domestic affairs, and impracticable to fuse them into one homogeneous community. To suit this state of facts a political system was devised two thousand years ago, and has since been perfected by many a wise statesman in many a famous State. It is known,

technically, as the Composite System, or Federalism; by German writers as *Bundesstaät.*
Like every political system, it suits only the
state of facts for which it was devised. To
apply it to any other state of facts, (as was in-
sanely attempted in France last year,) is to
misapply it. Indeed, more than most systems,
it needs caution in application. To what
state of facts does it apply? Let Mr. FREE-
MAN, the distinguished historian of the system,
answer; and we are the safer to take his answer
because it is given without reference to Ireland, and because his opinion, as expressed
in another place, would appear to be adverse
to Irish claims. 'The Federal System,' says
Mr. FREEMAN, 'requires a sufficient degree of
community in origin, or feeling, or interest, to
allow the members to work together up to a
certain point. It requires that there should
not be that perfect degree of community, or
rather identity, which allows the members to
be fused together for all purposes. When there
is no community at all Federalism is inappropriate: the cities or States had better remain wholly independent. When commu-

nity rises into identity Federalism is equally inappropriate; the cities or states had better both sink into the counties of a kingdom. But in the intermediate set of circumstances .. Federalism is the true solvent. It gives as much union as the members need, and not more than they need.'* Such is the canon of fitness for Federal Government which the historian of Federalism lays down; and he is in substantial accord with every great authority on the subject. But it is evident that the English language could not summarise with more neatness the very state of facts we have been considering. Ours is precisely 'the intermediate set of circumstances' for which political philosophy prescribes Federalism as 'the true solvent;' and Federalism is precisely what the HOME GOVERNMENT ASSOCIATION proposes for that state of facts. I submit, therefore, that it is not the Federal proposal that needs to be justified in the face of science: it is the resistance to it that needs such justification.

As to the existing system, I know not what

---

* *Hist. Fed. Govt.*, vol. i. p. 109.

scientific defence can be made for it. If it worked well it might be justified, like any other well-working anomaly ; but, failing this apology, it has none. It defeats that which Guizot's celebrated maxim declares to be the special end and sole 'raison d'être' of representative government, namely, that the people should have the constant direction and effectual control of their own government, and should be ruled, not according to abstract principles, but according to the wants generated by their own special circumstances. It violates the fundamental politico-philosophic principle that every organised society has a right to freedom in handling its own domestic affairs. It fails by the first criterion of good government, viz. : the degree in which it tends to increase the sum of good qualities in the governed, because it is only by exercising some degree of self-government that a community gains political experience, tolerance, and self-control. It is a clear case of over-centralization, because it aims at forcing a system suitable only for a homogeneous community on two communities

which are clearly not homogeneous, and because its practical result is the subjection of
the domestic affairs of one distinct, idiosyncratic, and ancient community to the management of another community which, admittedly, does not understand these affairs and
has not time to attend to them, which, confessedly, has failed to manage them to the
satisfaction of anyone concerned, and whose
interference in these domestic affairs at all is
notoriously at variance with the deepest
national instincts of the subject people.

III.

But thoughtful and cautious enquirers will
be slow to adopt an important political proposal, even though it appear to be what
impartial common sense would suggest and
sound political philosophy prescribe for the
state of facts in question. Such an enquirer
would still pause and ask, Was this plan tried
elsewhere? If so, where? How did it work?

The abundance of the evidence in favour of
the Federal proposal, considered from this point

of view, constitutes the only difficulty in dealing with it in a paper like this. To answer fully would be to recapitulate some of the noblest pages in the history of the world. As it is we can only take a few instances, and indicate the general results.

In ancient times the most conspicuous example of the Federal system was the famous Achaian League. So dear was local legislative and administrative freedom to the Hellenic mind, that in 'the golden prime' of Greece nearly every great city was a state, and nearly every state was absolutely independent. But when Athens fell isolated states were too weak to withstand the power of Macedonia. Then arose the need of combining for all purposes of common defence and general administration, without sacrificing the control by each community of its own domestic affairs. This was accomplished by the Achaian League. It enabled each state to retain its legislative and administrative independence in all that concerned its own exclusive affairs; but it massed them all for all common purposes into one common

state, with one common legislature, magistracy, and army. The League was not only
successful in fulfilling its original purpose,
but it arrested Hellenic decadence for centuries, and gave to a large part of Greece a
' second summer' of peace, freedom, and
orderly government.*

Amongst many mediæval examples, let us
take that of the United Provinces of the
Netherlands. Here was another case where
it was necessary that several states should
stand as one for all common purposes, and
yet impracticable that all should be fused into
a homogeneous and centralised state. The
problem was easily, wisely, and successfully
solved by the Federal arrangement. The
sturdy states combined for every purpose for
which combination was useful. In the face
of Spain and the world they constituted but
one sovereign state, with one army and administration, under one sovereign authority ; but
they continued distinct and free for all other
purposes. There was no rude levelling of

* See Freeman, *Hist. Fed. Gov.*, vol. i. Grote's *Hist. Greece*,
vol. x.

local rights before a central rule ; no clumsy
cutting of all coats to one pattern ; no haughty
dominance of one community over the home
affairs of another.   Each state lived under the
domestic laws which none but it had made.
The arrangement succeeded.   Thus united and
yet thus free, the Netherlanders held the sand-
banks which their industry had made rich
against Spain when Spain was almost mistress
of the world.   They prospered long and well.
Their wealth was the envy of kings.   Their flag
was borne bravely age after age on sea and
land.*   Submerged by the French Revolution,
an attempt was made to fuse them into one
centralised state.   After a brief trial, the experiment failed.   The country was separated into
two independent kingdoms.   And now, in our
own days, some of the leading statesmen of
both kingdoms are considering the wisdom
of resuming the Federal tie which worked so
well in the old times, and seem likely not
only to verify, but to anticipate, the prediction
of LAING that 'these two little states would
come together again . . . not as one mo-

* See Motley's *Hist. United Netherlands*.

narchy, but as independent states federally united under one general Government.'*

Switzerland presents an instance of Federalism, commencing in the earliest mediæval times, and lasting, with varying extent and constitution, but with nearly unbroken order, to our own day, when it is as gallant, as prosperous, though not as wise, as ever. Here is another clear case of 'a sufficient degree of community to allow the members to work together up to a certain point' without 'that perfect degree of community, or rather identity, which allows the members to be fused together for all purposes.' The perils of their position forbade them being disunited. The diversity of their habits, religions, and customs, rendered centralization impossible. Federalism proved to be 'the true solvent.' It left each community free to manage its own private affairs. It combined all in one state for all common purposes.†
The very troubles and dangers of the Swiss Federation are instructive. In the affair of

---

* *Notes of a Traveller*, p. 25.
† Wheaton's *International Law*, 75.

the Sonderbund (1847) the central authority encroached on cantonal independence by intermeddling with the domestic educational arrangements of certain states. Quite apart from the merits of the particular question, it is now clear that such interference was a violation of the Federal pact, and one of those successes which are worse than defeats.* In this present year the 'Internationale,' defeated at Paris, has turned its attention to Switzerland, and is labouring to follow up the movement of 1847 by an effort for the total abolition of cantonal rights and the complete centralization of Swiss institutions.† This is, of course, being firmly, and I trust, successfully, resisted. Thus we find the Commune striving for centralization, and the friends of order maintaining ' Home Rule.'

The United States of America afford another example of the successful combination of local self-government with Imperial unity. Nearly a century ago a few remote and despised colonies set up for themselves. We can still read in the quaint pages of the

---

* *Annuaire des Deux Mondes*, 1850.
† See 'Internationale Programme,' *Times*, August 30, 1871.

Federalist how the able men who framed the American constitution approached their work; with what amplitude of knowledge, with what shrewd insight, with what subtle discrimination. It was clearly the interest of all the states to be one commonwealth. It was no less clearly their interest that each should manage its own domestic affairs. Ignorant or violent politicians would have disregarded one or other of these cardinal requirements; but these sound and sagacious statesmen accepted and reconciled them both.* Each state was left free in what concerned itself only; all were made subject to a common power in whatever concerned all collectively. I need not dwell on the result. The American political system, like all political systems, has its defects, its perils, and its abuses; but no reasonable critic will contend that its advantages, successes, and safeguards do not incalculably outweigh them. Under it these few remote and despised colonies have grown into the very greatest community of modern times. Its very abuses

---

* *Federalist*, Nos. 9, 21, &c. 'Articles of Confederation,' vi.

generally arise (as in the case of the New
York frauds *), not out of the system itself,
but out of divergences from it. The se-
cession grew out of such a divergence;
and the tremendous effort by which the
union was restored shows that, in America at
least, ' Home Rule ' does *not* ' mean separation.' Nay, if we are to believe the shrewdest
and most philosophical of all critics of the
American constitution, it is *because* of Home
Rule that separation is impossible. ' In
great centralized states,' says M. DE TOCQUE-
VILLE, ' the legislator is obliged to impart a
character of uniformity to the laws which
does not always sanction the diversity of
customs and of districts, and the population is
obliged to conform to the exigencies of legislation since legislation cannot adapt itself to
the exigencies of the population. This is the
cause of endless trouble. But this disadvantage does not exist in Federations. It is
impossible to imagine how much the division
of legislative labour contributes to the well-
being of each of the states which compose

* See *Pall Mall Gazette*, Sept. 27, 1871.

the union. In these small communities, which are never agitated by the desire of aggrandizement or the cares of self-defence, all public authority and private energy are employed on internal amelioration . . . and the American citizen defends the union, because in defending it he defends the increased prosperity and freedom of his own district.'* May it not be worth considering whether such ' silken cords of love ' and such strong bonds of interest might not be better safeguards for the Imperial unity of these kingdoms than the artificial trammels of unsuitable centralization, or the apprehensions with which the strength of one community inspires the weakness of the other ?

Sweden and Norway supply another illustration. In 1814 it was clearly desirable that both countries should be united : it was no less clear that they were not sufficiently identical to be fused together for all purposes. What to do ? Separate ? That would have been ruin. Centralise ? That would have been impracticable. Sacrifice Norwegian in-

* *Démocratie en Amérique*, c. vii. pp. 186–7.

dependence to Swedish dominance ? That would not have been tolerated. Combine for common purposes, but retain internal independence ? This was done, and the arrangement has proved both permanent and beneficial.*

The Austro-Hungarian arrangement is a recent case. For nearly a hundred years Austria had been striving to convert the several states of the Empire into one centralised community, and, in particular, to make Hungarian institutions give way to German rule. This effort has been made with the utmost force, persistence, and perseverance by Kaiser after Kaiser, by statesman after statesman, generation after generation. It resulted in nothing but local disaffection and Imperial weakness. After the stern lesson learned at Sadowa it was completely given up. The Reichstag, or National Hungarian Parliament, was restored, and given supreme control of all the domestic affairs of Hungary. Imperial affairs were confided to an Imperial Assembly in which Hungary is duly represented.

* See Laing's *Travels in Norway.*

Of course no one can prophesy what will be the ultimate result. But every observer testifies that hitherto the change has been most beneficial. 'Before 1867,' says an able and well informed writer in the *Quarterly Review*, 'Hungary was a discontented province kept in order by German troops : it is now the most contented and patriotic part of the Empire.' *

Still more recently, Prince BISMARK and his astute colleagues have given an unexpected adhesion to the Federal principle in framing the new Imperial German Constitution. It is not indeed a true *Bundesstaät*, but it is much nearer to it than its predecessor the North German Confederation. Each state preserves a large portion of its autonomy ; all are represented in the *Bundesrath*, or Imperial Federal Assembly. So respectful are even these iron conquerors of the rights of subordinate communities, so cautious to avoid the error of coercing all to lie on the Procrustes bed of one centralised sys-

* See Art. 'Austria since Sadowa,' *Quarterly Review*, July, 1871.

tem, that it is expressly provided that the
representatives of one community are not to
vote on what concerns only the domestic
affairs of another community.*

In the discussion of this matter it seems to
be almost forgotten that the principle of
Federalism has been repeatedly and expressly
accepted by the Imperial Parliament, and is
now at work satisfactorily in various parts
of the Queen's dominions.   But such is the
fact.   'It is now a fixed principle,' says Mr.
MILL, 'of the policy of Great Britain, pro-
fessed in theory and faithfully adhered to in
practice, that her colonies of European race
should equally with the parent country possess the fullest measure of internal self-government. . . . Each is governed by its own
legislature and executive, and has full control
over its own affairs.'† Nor is the self-government nominal merely.   'It is,' as Mr. MILL
says, 'faithfully adhered to in practice.' 'The
veto of the Crown and of Parliament, though
nominally reserved, is only exercised, (and that

* *Verfassung des Deutschen Reiches*, Art. xiii.
† Mill's *Representative Government*, p. 131.

very rarely,) on questions which concern the Empire and not solely the particular colony. British Ministers almost invariably respect the independence of the local legislatures.'* Thus, in his celebrated New Zealand despatch of March 1869, Lord GRANVILLE's argument is expressly based on the principle that an independent people should be left to manage its own affairs, and that the authority of its Government should not be interfered with. Nor is this all. The British Ministers and the Imperial Parliament have lately favoured the principle, that colonies should not only be self-governed, but should form Federal arrangements between themselves. Last session Parliament was discussing a project for the Federation of the Leeward Islands, proposed by Sir BENJAMIN PINE, one of the most experienced Colonial servants of the Crown. Last year letters patent were issued by Her Majesty, appointing the Honourable GAVAN DUFFY and others Royal Commissioners, to consider and report on the necessity of a Federal union of the Australian Colonies. In 1867, a complete

* Ibid. p. 132.

scheme of Federation and Home Rule was
passed through Parliament for the British
North American Provinces, and the rights and
jurisdictions of central and provincial legislatures were minutely discriminated by statute.*
This system has worked excellently. Each
province manages its own domestic affairs :
whatever is of common interest to all is
entrusted to the action of a central legislation. ' The immediate effect ' (says a well
known writer in the *Contemporary Review*)
' has been to facilitate the settlement of
questions which were previously sources of
angry recrimination. In the province of
Quebec, a legislature representing an enor-
mously excessive constituency of Roman
Catholics, conceded to the Protestant minority what probably they never would have
yielded when Upper and Lower Canada were
united under one Government. Each legislature, relieved of the more general subjects
of legislation and debate, is now vigorously
pursuing the policy of development, extending
education, promoting colonization, roads and
railways, and encouraging immigration.'†

* 30 Vic. c. III.   † *Contemporary Review*, Jan. 1871.

Everyone knows how Canadian loyalty re-vived with Canadian freedom : how an Irish ' rebel' of 1848 became a faithful Minister of the Crown ; and how the venerable PAPINEAU volunteered to fight for the unity of the Empire.

The Channel Islands and the Isle of Man supply illustrations of self-government recon-ciled with British Imperial unity of a far more ancient and still more interesting and in-structive character. By race, religion, and geographical position, (as Mr. MILL points out,) Guernsey and Jersey belong less to Great Britain than to France. Their possession by France would have made them fearful thorns in the side of Great Britain. How have they been reconciled ? By forced centralization ? By rough and clumsy over-ruling of their distinctive ways, rights, habits, and interests ? By contemptuous disregard of their claims to self-government ? By being told that they were merely English counties ? Not at all. Their internal affairs are almost ex-empted from English statute-law. They are allowed complete control over these affairs; they manage them well; their trade flourishes; their agricultural system is a model; their people are content; and Imperial unity has no stauncher friends in the Queen's dominions. Still more striking is the case of Man. Here is an island of little more than fifty thousand inhabitants, lying in the very heart of the Irish Sea. Like Ireland, it is geographically distinct from Great Britain. Like Ireland, its population is chiefly of Celtic origin. Like Ireland, it was formerly independent, but gradually fell under the dominance of its big neighbour. Like Ireland, it has distinctive ways, habits, character, interests, and rights. Like Ireland, it was for centuries more or less hostile to Great Britain. Like Ireland, it claimed distinct independent existence. Like Ireland, its possession by any foreign power would be almost fatal to the Empire. How has a 'modus vivendi' been established? Why is it that one never hears of 'the Manx question?' Why is a breath of disloyalty never heard from the Isle of Man? Because in dealing with it Great Britain has acted with sound common sense, with statesmanlike magnanimity, in accordance with politico-philosophic principles and with the wants and ways of the human heart. It did not attempt to override Manx rights. It did not laugh to scorn Manx claims to separate civil existence. It did not treat as homogeneous that which was distinct. It did not clumsily and blunderingly force centralization where centralization was inappropriate. It did the contrary of all these. It left Man its individual civil existence, its ancient local Parliament, and full control over its own internal affairs. Man is governed by its own laws made by the three Estates of its own isle.*

It may be objected that not one of these cases is precisely the same as that now under discussion. I submit that this objection is untenable. No case in history is precisely the same as any other case. It may as well be objected to the results of medical experience that no man's constitution is precisely the same as any other man's. For that matter, scarcely anything is precisely the same as

* See Thwaite's *Isle of Man*, p. 54.

anything else. If this objection were to be
held good, history would be worthless, experience useless. But it is not so. Honest,
earnest, and patient enquirers will study the
past as guidance for the future, and find the
true points of identity underlying diversities.
In all the instances we have been considering
there will be found such points of identity
with each other and with the relative circumstances of Great Britain and Ireland. In all
there will be found to have been a clear need
of union for common purposes. In all there
will be found to have been equally clear
obstacles to complete centralization. And
in all the reasonable requirements of Imperial
unity were reconciled with the reasonable
requirements of local freedom by the very
system with which it is now proposed to meet
the same requirements here.

I cannot conclude this section without quot-
ing the weighty judgment in which the acutest
and most thoughtful observer of modern political systems sums up his opinion on the subject :
and I beg my reader to note with what
curious exactness the results of Mr. LAING's

experience tally with those of Mr. FREEMAN's
philosophical enquiries. ' Wheresoever,' says
Mr. LAING, ' the rights and advantages of one
mass of population, their prosperity, industry,
well-being, property, national benefits of soil,
situation and climate, their manners, language, religion, nationality in spirit or prejudice, are set aside and sacrificed to those of
another mass . . . the principle of Federalism seems a more natural and just principle
of general government, theoretically considered, than this forced centralization. No
rights or advantages of any of the parts are
sacrificed in Federalism, for nothing is centralised but what is necessary for the external
defence, safety, and welfare of all the parts.
The peculiar internal welfare of each part
according to its own peculiar internal circumstances, physical and moral, according to its
own political idiosyncracy, is in its own
keeping, in its own internal legislative and
administrative powers. As civilization, peace,
and industry acquire an influence in the
affairs of mankind . . . the superiority of
this system will probably be acknowledged

by all civilised populations. . . . Nature forbids by the unalterable differences of soil, climate, situation, and natural advantages, or by the equally unalterable moral differences between people and people, that one government can equally serve all, be equally suited to promote the utmost good of all. Federalism involves a principle more akin to natural, free, and beneficial legislation . . . appears more reasonable and suitable to the well-being of society, and appears to be that towards which civilised and educated society is naturally tending.' *

I now conclude my observations on the theoretical aspect of the present proposal. Its practical advantages may or may not be doubtful : these we shall consider in the next chapter. Practical difficulties may or may not outweigh all theoretical advantages ; this we shall consider in a subsequent chapter. But I submit that, looking only to the theory of the matter, reviewing the train of thought we have been considering, and the various

* *Notes of a Traveller*, pp. 25, 26, 27.

other trains of thought of which we have only
suggested the commencements, the conviction
will gradually gain force in honest, open, and
well-balanced minds, that, theoretically at
least, the proposal of the HOME GOVERNMENT
ASSOCIATION is sound and reasonable. I
submit that the more gravely, acutely, and
soberly the matter is considered the more
such a conviction will grow. When two
islands are united by many ties and have many
interests in common, yet are geographically,
historically, socially, and actually distinct
and different, common sense would say :
combine for what is of common interest ;
manage separately what only concerns each
individually ; never cease to hold hands
together against the world, but let neither
ever try to lord it over the domestic affairs
of the other ; co-operate in everything for
which co-operation is useful, but do not
blindly and clumsily insist that one community must wear the social garments and
work by the political machinery intended for
another and quite different community ; be
assured that between nations, as between men,

true and lasting union can exist only on the understanding that each respect the individuality of the other. When a legislative experiment has been tried for seventy years and has not worked to the satisfaction of any one concerned, it is time to consider whether it may . not be advantageously modified. Where you have evidence in every page of the history of six hundred years, and fresh evidence in nearly every morning's newspaper, that there is a deepseated instinct of nationality in the inmost hearts of a people, common sense would say : respect that instinct ; do not persist in rubbing against the grain ; see what you can do to reconcile a feeling so natural and so healthy with Imperial requirements, and make it the friend, not the foe, of the Commonwealth. When a legislative assembly is notoriously worked almost beyond endurance, and yet is obliged to neglect the most urgent matters, educational, social, naval, and military,—matters that concern the inmost life of the population—matters that concern its external strength and the very

continuity of its existence—common-sense
would say : divide the labour; do not, like
some arrogant and fussy heads of commercial
houses, insist on doing everybody's business ;
permit what concerns Ireland exclusively to
be managed by Irishmen. I submit that
these dictates of common-sense are ratified by the plainest canons and the ripest
results of politico-philosophic enquiry ; that
the very system proposed is precisely the one
which political philosophy prescribes as ' the
true solvent ' for the very case in hand ; the
case, namely, where between countries there
is ' a sufficient degree of community in origin
or feeling or interest to allow the several
members to work together up to a certain
point,' and yet ' not that perfect degree of
community, or rather identity, which allows
the several members to be fused together for
all purposes.' There may be practical reasons
why in this case the canons of political
philosophy should be disregarded; but in
this case, for some reason or for no reason,
we *are* disregarding them, and persisting in
substituting for the system which in such a

case political philosophy recommends a system which it condemns. Lastly : is it not difficult to reflect on the vast number of instances in which our problem has been satisfactorily solved, and yet persist in maintaining that for us it is insoluble ; that all the wit, wisdom, and sagacity of these two great and famous islands are inadequate to find for them any satisfactory 'modus vivendi' ; that if we are not to sink into Scylla we must fall into Charybdis ; that for us there is no middle-term between a brutal separation and a no less brutal centralization?

CHAPTER IV.

What Practical Advantages are expected from it?

THEORETICALLY, then, it seems clear that the proposed system is the right one. Let us now consider its practical aspect. Theories, it may be said, are good in their way; but politics are matters of practical expediency, and we should like to have plainly stated what practical advantages are expected to be derived from it.

This is a perfectly fair question, yet I conceive it might receive a perfectly fair answer in three short sentences from one of Mr. GRANT DUFF's thoughtful and well-informed *Elgin Speeches* : 'First listen,' says Mr. DUFF, ' to the teachings of science and philosophy. Then work out the results painfully and slowly. This is the only true practicality.'*

* *Elgin Speeches*, p. 260.

If, as the considerations in the last chapter would indicate, this proposal be theoretically right, we may be assured that it will not prove to be practically wrong.

In one of Mr. MATHEW ARNOLD's able papers on 'Liberty and Authority,' he elucidates, with his own charming perspicuity, the too-much-forgotten truth that political institutions of all kinds are but pieces of machinery for working out the public welfare. Now, if in working out our public welfare we have been employing a political machinery which common sense, political philosophy, and experience prove to be unsuitable, is it necessary to demonstrate in detail the advantage of rectifying our error, and getting the right machine instead of the wrong one?

If a competent man of business were somehow superseded in the management of his affairs by a committee of good-natured but somewhat supercilious and very busy neighbours, would it be necessary to demonstrate in detail the practical advantage of letting him mind his own business—business which no one could understand so well, in which no one could feel so deep an interest, as himself?

But let us look into the matter more closely.

If there be any one thing about which it is safe to say that all the civilised world and all political thinkers are agreed, it is that, ordinarily speaking, a community gets on better when it manages its own affairs, than when those affairs are managed for it by another community, just as, ordinarily speaking, a man gets on better when he has the management of his own affairs, than when he is in bondage or tutelage to any one else. This thought underlies all the praises of civil liberty that ever were said or sung. It is, beyond doubt, a true thought. Unless the community or the man be mad they know their own business better than anyone else can know it. Unless they be utter incapables, they will do it better than anyone else can do it. Unless they be sneaks, they will feel as an intolerable grievance the pretension of anyone else to supersede them in it. Keep a man in such bondage or tutelage, and you will make him a milksop; all inventiveness,

all brightness of genius, all force of character,
all aspiration to achievement will die out in
him; no such man ever does any real good
for himself or anyone else. Keep a community in such bondage and tutelage, and
you emasculate it for all good purposes and
put it in 'the way of temptation' to all bad
ones; public spirit, self-reliance, self-control,
self-knowledge, national faith, national hope,
national charity will decline; no such community prospers, or ever yet really prospered
since the world began. But this is just the
position of the community which lives within
the four seas of Ireland. A large, intelligent
community, geographically, historically, and
actually distinct, it is denied the management
of its own affairs. These are virtually managed for it by Great Britain. It has a voice
in their management, no more. The practical control and ultimate government of the
domestic concerns of Ireland rest, not with
the Irish community, but with the community that lives in the neighbouring island,
or its representatives. The results which
generally follow so objectionable an arrange-

ment have followed here. How can a calm and candid enquirer resist the conclusion that it would be desirable to revert to the natural order of things, and restore to this distinct, ancient, and idiosyncratic community the control of its domestic affairs? Unless all the world, and all political thinkers, and all sagacious observers, and all orators and poets, have utterly deceived themselves as to the practical advantageousness of civil liberty, this restoration must be attended with the political advantages which ordinarily follow the possession of such liberty. I submit that this consideration alone is sufficient answer to the question at the head of this chapter. To a community, as to a man, rational liberty is the first of 'practical advantages.' Without it energy flags, enterprise fails, strength declines, life itself decays.

So far for principle : turn now to details. The more we examine them the clearer the matter becomes.

I suppose it will be admitted that for the efficient transaction of any legislative or administrative business there is one thing indisputably necessary, viz. TIME. Even in these high-pressure days we cannot escape from that old-fashioned requirement. As Mr. BRUCE lately put it, legislators can no more pass measures without time, than the Israelites could make bricks without straw. A legislator or administrator can work only a certain number of hours in the day or night, and can attend to them efficiently only by taking them one by one. But if there be any subject on which it may be said that all political parties just now agree, it is that the House of Commons has *not* time to do all the business thrown upon it. Nearly every leading statesman has called attention to this. So has nearly every leading organ of public opinion. Nearly every ministerial speech contains an apology, sometimes quite a pathetic one, for urgent national business left undone because of there not being time to do it. Grave thinkers hold that Parliamentary Government itself has arrived at a crisis in consequence of this practical difficulty. It is described as a state of ' chronic choke,' of incessantly recurring ' dead-lock.' It results

not only in total neglect of some of the most
urgent social and political questions—questions of life and death to individuals, and to
the Empire itself—but in the hasty, confused, and irregular treatment of such as are
dealt with. As to Irish questions, they were
for years, one might say for generations,
scarcely attended to at all. With rare exceptions, a ' mere Irish ' question was considered
a bore, to be laughed off, or counted out, or
dealt with in slipshod official fashion. In
later years the Imperial Parliament applied
itself to two great Irish questions with an
energy, a generosity, and a zeal which it
would be dishonour to forget or depreciate.
While this was being done the most urgent
English, Scotch, Indian, and Imperial business was necessarily neglected. Being done,
the deferred questions naturally and properly
claimed parliamentary attention. Thus Irish
business has been again shelved. Parliament
cannot be always at Irish business : yet Irish
business always demands attention. The noble
Chief Secretary had to withdraw even his Bill
respecting Labourers' Dwelling-houses ; and

as the Registrar-General tells us, half-a-million of Irish men and women, the men and women who really push the plough and wield the sickle, are left to live in what M. DE BEAUMONT termed 'huts of one room which an Esquimaux would despise.' 'During the last session,' says one of the ablest, if not the very ablest, of Irish members, 'there were many Irish Bills on the paper, and in scarcely a single instance did those come before the House until long after midnight, while in various instances they were hustled through at two o'clock, aye, and at three o'clock in the morning! No wonder,' he bitterly adds, 'that laws rushed through their different stages with a precipitancy which precludes the possibility of adequate consideration should be afterwards a puzzle to lawyers and an evil to the community.'* Now, in the name of common sense and right reason, what is the object of continuing a system so inconvenient to everybody concerned, and fraught with such peril to both islands? Why refuse to let local Irish business be transacted by

* Mr. Maguire, M.P., in *Cork Examiner*, Oct. 17, 1871.

Irish men, who will, at least, have time to attend to it, and who will have no other public business to attend to?

If there be one other requirement indisputably necessary for the efficient transaction of legislative business, it is KNOWLEDGE. All the talk in the world—nay, all the good intentions in the world, won't make up for the want of it. Now, candidly speaking, what does an ordinary English or Scotch member *know* about Ireland? Perhaps he does his best to find out about it; he has heard a lot of speeches, he has read several blue books, he has run over for a fortnight with introductions to the leading gentry, and he has taken care also to have a chat with the peasants and to see what the priests are like; but if he did not happen to be a Member of Parliament, who would really care a straw for his opinion on any local Irish question? Who would be guided by his judgment in any practical detail of Irish life? What is such dilettante hap-hazard information worth for practical purposes compared with the life-long acquaintance which every man has with the

affairs of his own community ? Why insist
that such local affairs must be administered
for the most part, and all really decisive conclusions respecting them arrived at, by men
who, however intelligent and estimable, *know*
scarcely anything about these affairs, and who,
amongst a hundred good qualities, are notoriously deficient in the aptitude for realizing
positions, appreciating facts, and understanding feelings to which they are unfamiliar ?
The blunders committed by eminent English
legislators and administrators, even in the
very topography of Ireland, are amongst the
traditional jokes of 'the House.' These may
have been accidental, but it cannot be acci-
dent that produces the honest, rueful, ever-
recurring complaint of English legislators
that they cannot, for the life of them, 'understand Ireland.' Why insist on their dealing
with subjects which they 'cannot understand ?'
The great authority of Mr. MILL appears to
be adverse to the proposal under discussion ;
but it is Mr. MILL himself who teaches us that
' it is always under great difficulties, and very
imperfectly, that a country can be governed

by foreigners, even when there is no extreme
disparity in habits and ideas between the
rulers and the ruled. Foreigners do not feel
with the people. They cannot judge by the
light in which a thing appears to their own
minds, or the manner in which it affects their
feelings, how it will affect the feelings or
appear to the minds of the subject population.
What a native of the country of average
practical ability knows as it were by instinct
they have to learn slowly, and, after all,
imperfectly, by study and experience.'*

Again : consider all the legislative and
administrative work which remains to be done
for Ireland, and which, under the present
system, must be done, if done at all, by men
who have not time to attend to it, who know
scarcely anything about it, and who complain
that they 'cannot understand' it. To intelligent Irishmen there are few things more
strange than the often repeated demand :
What are your 'grievances?' Civilised communities generally deem deprivation of the
control of their own domestic affairs the

* *Representative Government*, p. 135.

greatest of all 'grievances.' But suppose this were not so, is it not a 'grievance' that nearly all the national legislative work of the country is left undone or but half done, that nearly every national interest is neglected, that the national resources are squandered, that the national wealth, intellectual and material, is directed into other channels, and that nearly the whole of Irish society from top to bottom needs to be reconstructed? Every Irishman with his eyes open knows that this is the actual state of things ; but let us verify it by considering the matter in detail.

Take the Agricultural Interest. In a country almost exclusively agricultural this is necessarily the main dependence. In many countries, (as Mr. MAGUIRE points out,) it is considered so important that the care of it constitutes a special department of the state under a special ministry. In other countries, (as Mr. THORNTON points out,) great agricultural colleges are planted in every city, and a school of agriculture in every village. What is the condition of Irish agriculture? Let the first authority on such subjects in Europe answer. M. LEONCE DE LAVERGNE told us a few years ago that 'l'imagination s'effraie quand on essaie de mesurer ce qui manque à un pays dans cet état,' * and that it would take 320,000,000*l.* to put Irish land into the same condition as that of other civilised countries. Things have improved since ; but the improvement is trivial compared with what remains to be done. And what has the legislature done for Irish agriculture? Until last year it allowed it to languish under a system which everybody now admits to have been indefensible, and it resisted with scorn every attempt at reform. It still leaves half-a-million of labourers in ' huts of one room that an Esquimaux would despise.' It leaves drainage, the great requirement of Irish soil and climate, almost undone. 'And whilst millions of the public money are expended on other parts of the United Kingdom, those great works which only government can deal with, such as the deepening of river-beds and the arterial drainage of large districts, are

* *Écon. rur. de l'Angleterre,* p. 385.

nearly altogether neglected.'* Of the twenty
millions of arable Irish acres it leaves more
than two-thirds either half tilled or in pasture.
It leaves over a million of Irish acres that are
capable of cultivation without any cultivation whatever. It does not effectively provide agricultural instruction. The very existence of the present system of centralised
government draws away from Irish agriculture those who ought to be its patrons and
its chiefs. An Irish proprietor like Lord
BANDON, living on his estates and applying
himself to the advancement of his tenantry,
is an exception indeed. The able organ of
the Conservatives in the south of Ireland—
the *Cork Constitution*—(though no favourer
of Home Rule,) truly tells the reason. 'The
effect of centralization on this country,' it
says, ' is gradually to reduce us to the condition of a mere outlying farm for the supply of the English markets . . . As to all
classes above the farming class there will be

* *Ireland, Industrial, Political and Social*, by John Nicholas
Murphy, p. 91 (Longmans and Co.) : a repertory of reliable
and admirably selected information which every student of the
' Irish Question ' should have in his library.

less and less every year to tempt them to reside in Ireland. A few favoured localities such as Dublin and Cork may resist the tendency for a longer or shorter time, and Belfast, owing to its linen manufacture, will probably continue to increase both in population and in wealth. But these are exceptional cases : Dublin and Cork may not remain exceptions long.' * Would it not be practically advantageous to Ireland to check this centralization, to give Irish proprietors their proper places in Irish national life, to get up a real system of agricultural instruction such as exists in most self-governed communities, and to encourage Irishmen to consult together for the development of Irish resources and the promotion of Irish agricultural interests ?

Take the Manufacturing Interest. What is its condition ? Except linen, porter, and whiskey, there are scarcely any manufactories in Ireland. Almost all the manufactured articles used in Ireland, save these, are British or foreign products. What has the

* *Cork Constitution*, June 8, 1871.

Imperial Legislature done for the Irish manufacturing interest? At first it passed laws
to repress it; having repealed those laws it
neglects it. In nearly every continental
country, as Lord DERBY lately pointed out,
the state has instituted, endowed, and ac-
tively superintends a system of technical
instruction by which workmen are gratui-
tously taught drawing, modelling, carving,
chemistry, and mechanics; and to this state-
aid his lordship attributes the growing superiority of continental manufactories. In
France there is a school of technical art in
every important town. In Germany there is
a complete system of technical training from
the *Realschulen* of the villages to the Poly-
technic Universities of Berlin and Stuttgardt.
In West Flanders the state instructs yearly
two thousand boys in weaving. Geneva has
immense schools for teaching watchmaking.
Thrifty, self-governed little Zurich maintains
the best technical university in the world, in
which everything that is most valuable in the
arts and manufactures of other countries is
taught by the most competent teachers any-

where procurable in the best manner that experience can suggest, and with all the aid that the best material appliances can afford. Steady, self-governed Wurtemberg has provided within the last twenty years for the technical instruction of the population, (not so large as that of Munster,) one university, two colleges of the first rank, and more than a hundred high trade-schools, and has thus conquered a place in the front rank of the manufacturing industry of the world.* Is there any country more in need of technical instruction than Ireland? Are there any people possessing more aptitude for receiving it, more quickness of intelligence, more fineness of touch, more sureness of hand, than our people? Yet in Ireland technical instruction is almost unknown. Even our little poplin manufacturers cannot get any reasonable facility. 'We had great hopes,' says an eminent poplin manufacturer, quoted by Mr. MURPHY, ' that some steps would have

---

* See, for further details, Mr. Scott Russell's important work on *Systematic Technical Education* (Bradbury and Evans). Also Mr. W. T. Thornton's admirable paper in the *Cornhill Magazine* of September last.

been taken by Government to redeem the promise of its predecessors to establish an institute of science and art. Nothing can be more injurious to every branch of art manufacture than the want of such an institute. The Irish designer, admitted to be brilliant and fertile in his imagination, finds his genius cramped, by being unable to resort to such collections of artistic models as are so freely at the disposal of the British and continental workmen.' *

Take Education. What is its condition? Primary education is defective in principle and in practice. Intermediate education is entirely left to voluntary enterprise and is notoriously imperfect. University education may be said to exist only for a favoured few. In public we are assured that all will be made right when our representatives present 'an united demand;' as if the representatives of any country were ever 'united,' about anything! In private we are whispered that all would be right only for the 'Scotch members;' as if it were reasonable that 'Scotch members' should dictate how

* *Ireland, Industrial, Political and Social*, p. 47.

Irishmen are to educate their own children !
Surely the remedy is to let those whom it
concerns settle the matter amongst themselves. Those who prefer to have their children religiously educated would be enabled
to do so. Those who prefer the absence of
religious instruction would be free to exercise their preference. And the whole country
would receive the advantages of the thorough
educational training which prevails in most
self-governed countries, and which is every
day becoming of more importance in 'the
battle of life.'

Take the Railway Interest. What a muddle ! Five hundred directors at cross purposes about sixty-six enterprises, that in
England would be all managed by a single
board, and on the continent by a single official :
high rates, low dividends, inferior accommo-
dation, conflicting time-tables, jarring interests, enormous parliamentary expenses,
progress almost suspended before the work is
half done, or the public wants half supplied,
remonstrance blandly bowed out with the
assurance that the matter will be attended to
as soon as 'the state of public business' per-

mits ; yet five years ago the admission : ' I
know of no method by which a boon could
be conferred on Ireland so comprehensive in
its operations, so impartial, so free from the
taint of suspicion of ministering to any particular interest or the views or convenience of
any particular class, one affecting the whole
population and all conditions without distinction, and that would be so universal in its
effect, as the better development of the Railway System of Ireland.'* Mr. GLADSTONE is
not to blame for not having conferred the
boon he intended and appreciated so well.
He cannot attend to everything. The ' state
of public business ' must undoubtedly be considered. But why not refer the matter to
those who have time to attend to it, who
know all about it, and whose interest it is to
set it right ? We know with what a cheap,
orderly, well-paying, and well-worked system
the little Belgian Parliament has supplied
the little Belgian Kingdom, and how
shrewdly every Swiss Canton sees after its
own railway interests.

* Mr. Gladstone, on Mr. Gregory's Motion in 1866.

The Aberdeen joke about Irish fisheries has occasioned much comment. After all, one should not take ' au grand sérieux ' a passing pleasantry. If Mr. GLADSTONE had time to look into the matter, he would be the first to rectify an almost obvious rhetorical slip. The fact is that Scotland, virtually controlling as an independent community its own affairs, wisely and munificently fostered its fishery interests by splendid grants, and that in Ireland, deprived as it is of any effective control of its own affairs, such interests were neglected, and such grants refused. Our clever Scotch friends might well smile at the eloquent Premier's compliment to their ' self-reliance' if they remembered that since 1800 this self-reliance was supplemented and developed by state aid to the extent of one million and a quarter pounds sterling more than Irish fisheries received for the same period, and that at present close on sixteen thousand pounds is annually spent by the state in the promotion of Scotch fisheries, while Ireland does not receive quite one thousand pounds for the same purpose ; that in Ireland, notwithstanding reiterated recommendations of Royal and Parliamentary commissions, grants, or even loans on good security, to Irish fishermen are peremptorily refused, and the provisions for advancing money for Irish piers and harbours are worked in such a niggardly and obstructive manner as to be almost valueless. The Irish Parliament of 1782 was far from being a model institution; but it looked well after this important Irish interest. In 1783 the Irish House of Commons voted 22,000l. for the advancement of Irish fisheries. In every fishing village there still lingers the tradition of ante-union prosperity. After the union, the Irish fisheries became almost extinct. They are now being revived, but they certainly want the judicious encouragement which every self-governed state takes care to render to so important a branch of its national industry.*

A self-governed community is generally on the alert, not only to encourage old industries, but to develop new ones. Under the present

* See Report of Select Committee on Irish Fisheries, 1867, p. 306; also Report of Coast and Deep Sea Fisheries in Ireland, 1870, p. 30.

system, this is almost as much neglected in Ireland as it probably is in Timbuctoo. Thus instruction in flax culture is left, for the most part, to private benevolence ; and the cultivation of tobacco is positively forbidden.

Irish legal affairs share the neglect and confusion of most departments of the Irish public service. The Bankruptcy and Insolvency law has been in a muddle for years. Facilities for land registration and land transfer, though requested by the leading proprietors and the most eminent judges, have been only imperfectly afforded. The grand-jury system is in confusion. Even the system of recovery of small debts is full of practical anomalies. Who is to set all this right ? What do English or Scotch members know of these local matters ? When will the Imperial Parliament have time to consider them at all, seeing that matters of the most urgent importance to the very existence of England and of the Empire await settlement ?

As to professional life, I may be permitted to quote the impartial testimony of the

able Cork Conservative Journal above men-
tioned :—' There is hardly an intellectual
profession in Ireland which is not at this
moment threatened with extinction from the
centralizing mania. The medical profession
was threatened a few months ago by Mr.
Bruce's Bill, which would have compelled
every future medical practitioner in Ireland
to obtain his diploma at an examination in
London, and would have tended powerfully,
though indirectly, to compel our medical
students to receive their whole education
there. This Bill is not withdrawn, but only
deferred. The candidates for employment in
the civil service of India are all examined in
London, and it is with private grinders in
London that the bulk of Irish students receive
their training. An attempt was made early
in the present session to exclude from the
engineering service of India any candidate
who had not received his professional education at Cooper's Hill, Surrey; and although
this Bill was modified owing to the strenuous
opposition of a few Scotch and Irish members, still the mitigated Act that did pass the

House has already the effect of sensibly injuring the principal engineering schools in this country. The arrangement which compels every Irish law student to attend an English Inn of Court before he can be called to the bar has hitherto proved but little injurious to Ireland, because the English legal education has been a farce ; but the Bill to be introduced next session by Sir ROUNDELL PALMER, compelling all law students to attend lectures for two or three years in London, would have the effect of completely transferring the body of students from Irish places of education to the brand new London one. . . . England is making very serious endeavours to cultivate the taste of its population in the direction of the fine and ornamental arts, and accordingly magnificent collections are being gathered at Kensington to train the eye of the student, while professorships are amply endowed for his æsthetic culture. There is nothing worth mentioning done in this direction for Ireland. . . . The bulk of the art students of Ireland obtain their education in London. . . . The object seems to be to

concentrate in and about London the whole
governing, administrative, and intellectual
life of the United Kingdom. . . . The effect
is almost to extinguish intellectual, artistic,
and social life in this country.'*   However the
acute and well-informed writer may differ
with me as to the means of setting this right,
I heartily concur with him as to the practical
advantage of, by *some* means, ' defending our
local institutions and our native sources of
wealth ' from this devouring centralization.

Dispassionately and soberly reviewing these
considerations, it seems difficult to resist the
conclusion that the wisdom of the ages was
right in prescribing for a case like ours the
arrangement of a combined Imperial, and an
independent domestic, legislature : that the
experiment of centralization, and ' the assumption that Englishmen could legislate
better for the Irish than they could for themselves,' to which many of us clung so passion-
ately, were mistakes after all : that this
country, like every other civilised country,
would thrive best with civil liberty : that the

* *Cork Constitution*, June 8, 1871.

healthy impulse of freedom would be bene-
ficially felt thoughout all the complicated
relations of our national life, and would tend
to 'reconstruct, encourage, awaken, and
educate the whole of Irish society,'* and that
from such a change we might expect the most
important practical advantages to the various
interests which, under the present system, are
either neglected or injuriously affected. This
conviction is certainly gaining ground
amongst thoughtful, practical and experienced
people at both sides of the Irish Channel. I
might select a score of notable instances. But
I choose one : that of Sir GEORGE GREY,
one of the most experienced servants of
the Crown, and one of the ablest and most
clear-headed men in England. 'Give to
Ireland,' says Sir GEORGE, ' a State Legislature
and a State Executive in Dublin ; secure
thereby the residence of its ablest men in the
country ; open a fair field as ministers, legislators, orators, to its best and wisest men ;
afford, from the same source, as would necessarily and certainly be done, occupation to

* *Contemporary Review*, Jan. 1871.

Irish architects, sculptors, painters, and secure a resident aristocracy of worth, talent, and wisdom, and you will at the same time restore the wealth, trade and commerce of Dublin and Ireland. Dumb Ireland will then speak again. Half inanimate Ireland will again awaken to national life, and breathe the breath of hope and freedom. Whilst by again accustoming the Irish people to the management of their own affairs, and to the administrative duties of the highest order, a willing people will be educated in that political knowledge which will enable them to put an end to the ills which afflict them, the causes and cure of which none can understand so well as themselves.'*

So far for advantages to Ireland : let us now consider the advantages of the proposed change to Great Britain.

As I write the bright autumn weather is clouded with apprehensions of coming evil. Every day's news brings some gloomy prognostication or some alarming statement. Foreign journalists appear to have come to a

* *The Irish Land Question*, by Sir George Grey, K.C.B., p. 19.

consensus that the British Empire is moribund. The Duke of SOMERSET tells us that our army cannot march and our ships cannot swim. Lord DERBY tells us that English workmen are being distanced in trade and manufactures. Count BLUMENTHAL is said to have 'laughed consumedly' at our autumn 'campaign.' Sir JOHN PAKINGTON discusses the causes that may lead to 'the ruin of England.' The trade 'strikes' assume great proportions. Daring 'Specials' explore and reveal the depths of pauperism, ignorance, vice and degradation in which vast masses of the British people are sunk. Complaints are heard on all sides of growing abuse and neglected reform. The army reform is only commenced. The navy reform is not even commenced. The relations between labour and capital grow worse and worse. Three hundred and fifty thousand miners are said to be in daily peril of their lives from dangers easily avoidable : yet the ' Mines Regulation Bill ' was withdrawn for want of time to consider it. Thousands are stated to perish annually because the recommendations of the Royal Sanitary Commission cannot be looked into. Of course there is much exaggeration in all this. Foreign journalists know as little of England as English 'members' do of Ireland. Statesmen use rhetorical figures. Social maladies will always more or less exist. English pluck, good sense, force of character, vast material resources and indomitable valour do not vanish in a day. I believe and I hope that for many a year, if not for centuries, to come, British freedom will be safe and the British Empire prosper. Nevertheless it would be idle to deny what every one admits and asserts, that the present state of affairs contains elements of great danger to England. Of all these elements of danger two appear by universal consent to be the most alarming, viz. (1) the neglect of social and administrative reforms, and (2) the disaffection of Ireland.

I submit that the proposal at present under discussion would be of the very utmost practical advantage in lessening these two evils. Let us consider them separately.

(1.) As to the neglect of social and administrative reform, what is the main cause of it? The very plethora of legislative and administrative business at Westminster to which we have so often alluded. ' If we ever fall as a nation' (Mr. HELPS makes Sir JOHN ELLESMERE say), ' it will be from too much pressure of business on our hands. We have so much to do with Ireland, with India, with our colonies, that it is hard work to find time for attending to those legislative measures which would greatly benefit our own people.'* ' The union of several Parliaments in one,' says Sir GEORGE GREY, ' charged with the minute special legislation upon so many points, in different countries, has thrown upon that one Parliament an amount of labour which it cannot perform. Hence its attention is distracted from its really important duties. Each determined party can force its own job through a distracted and bewildered assembly. Matters of the highest interest are neglected. All legislation is crude and unsatisfactory, and little or no explanation can be asked or afforded regarding the expenditure of the

* *Conversations on War and General Culture*, p. 259,

public funds, which are often squandered at the caprice of the party in power for the time. Whilst confused ministers frequently, indeed generally, new to their different offices, occupied with their duties to the Cabinet, in leading the two houses of the Legislature, and torn and worn by the enormous mass of duties of every kind thrown upon them in their respective offices, from the most important to the most trifling, in their effort to attend to all, are forced to neglect all, and the Government of the country has fallen into the hands of irresponsible clerks in the different offices, who care nothing for ruining ministers, or individual statesmen, if they promote views of their own, or advance the interests of their relations or friends. Hence is arising a disorder and an insubordination in the Empire such as has never before been seen.'*

Now, I put it to any man of common sense, is there any arrangement which would so tend to relieve this ' Parliamentary choke,'

---

* *Irish Land Question*, p. 18.

to lighten the strain on the legislative machine, to enable the most urgent Imperial interests to be attended to, and to set Englishmen and Scotchmen free to look after their own most pressing national affairs, as the proposed transference of Irish domestic business to an Irish legislative assembly? Is there a single English or Scotch member who has not been worried almost beyond endurance by the ever-recurring, never-ending, chamelion-like 'Irish question?' Moreover, would it not be a pleasure to every Briton to know that the domestic affairs of his country would be transacted by his own representatives, and no others? What can an average Irish member know about the internal affairs of England? What can his interference in them be other than a disturbing element in the equilibrium of parties, and an inconvenient interference in other people's domestic affairs?

(2.) As to the danger arising from Irish disaffection, it must be plain by this time that Great Britain can never be really safe while Ireland is discontented, and that utterly discontented Ireland will remain, so long as she is denied that control over her local affairs, which, as GRATTAN truly said, is the very ' essence of civil liberty,' and without the possession of which, as Sir GEORGE GREY admits, ' no nation can be contented, prudent or prosperous.' The concession of such control may have dangers of its own : these we shall discuss in the next chapter. But is there any danger so great as persistent defiance of the reasonable requirements, the ancient instinctive longings, and (as I venture to say,) the plain and certain rights, of the Irish community? Of old, GRATTAN warned PITT that in destroying the Irish Parliament he was ' pulling down one of the pillars of the British Empire,' and FOSTER predicted that its consequences might be the ' utter ruin ' of both countries. Let us be wise before it is too late. GOD made the two Islands neighbours, and separated them from all the world beside. History, race, kinship, social intercourses, individual friendship, knit them together by many a strong and tender tie. There can be no ' practical advantage ' so great to both as to make both friends, to end the miserable quarrels of the past, and to enable them both to enter on the future with combined strength and individual freedom.

CHAPTER V.

Objections Considered.

HAVING examined the Home Government Proposal in principle and detail, and considered certain arguments for believing it to be theoretically sound and practically advantageous, let us now frankly discuss the objections to it. Some of these objections have been incidentally dealt with as we went along; the rest I shall state here as clearly as I can. Most of them I hope will prove to be unfounded; several of them I know point to real difficulties and dangers. We shall candidly state and calmly consider both classes. Political proposals unattended by difficulties and dangers exist only in Utopia or in very boyish declamations. In real life every political proposal, and, for that matter, every political institution and constitution, has its difficulties and dangers. The most you can say of the best is, that its advantages considerably outweigh its disadvantages.

Objection I.

The arguments in favour of the Home Government Proposal may be plausible. Nevertheless it is a delusion. It cannot be seriously entertained at all. The reason is this : if Ireland were self-governed she would straightway attempt separation : such an attempt must either fail or succeed : if it failed it would leave Ireland bathed in the blood of her own sons ; if it succeeded it would dismember the Empire, plant a hostile State at England's weakest side, and establish a permanent base of operations for her enemies.

The dictates of humanity, therefore, combine with the instincts of self-preservation in forbidding English assent. All the plausibility in the world won't induce sensible men to do what will either ruin their neighbours or themselves. You may as well propose to restore the Heptarchy.

Answer.

There is danger that if Irishmen had the

control of their domestic affairs, they, or some
considerable portion of them, would seek
separation from Great Britain. There is also
danger that if Ireland be persistently refused
such control, they, or some considerable portion of them, will seek separation. The practical question is, which danger is the greater?
If conceding domestic autonomy to Ireland
would cause the greater danger of separation, or attempts at separation, Great Britain
would be unwise in making the concession.
If refusing it would cause the greater danger,
it would be folly to refuse.

To decide this question, let us see what are
the forces in Irish political life which resist
separation, what are the forces which tend to
it, and how the proposed concession and the
proposed refusal would affect these forces
respectively.

I am afraid it must be admitted that the
chief force which at present resists separation
is the physical one, i.e. the Army and Navy
at the disposal of the Imperial Government.
Under ordinary circumstances, at least, this
force renders separation impossible, and

attempts at it hopeless. Now the concession
of domestic autonomy to Ireland on the Federal plan, would not diminish it by a man,
or a ship, or a gun, or a shilling. It would
leave it at the disposal of the Imperial Government exactly as now; and the Imperial
Government would retain its full existing
powers to raise such force, to support it, to
augment it, to renew it, to direct it, to levy
taxes for it, and to enforce such taxation on
individual citizens.

But behind the Imperial physical force resisting separation, there is at present a vast
moral force in Ireland resisting it. All the
interests of property tend thus, so does nearly
all the educated intelligence of the country,
so does the common sense of men of business,
so do the million-fold personal relations of
kinship, friendship, and association between
individuals in both countries. Now it is evident that domestic autonomy would detract
nothing from this moral force. The interests
of property, the convictions of intelligence,
the conclusions of common sense, and the
relations of individuals, would be at least as

strongly against separation after such concession as before it. We may safely go a step
further, and admit that this moral force would
be likely to be increased by the adoption of
the Federal system. In such matters we can
only judge by experience and analogy. Experience and analogy certainly point in this
direction. DE TOCQUEVILLE told us long ago,
as an eventful history told us since, that it
is thus the Federal system has worked in
America, and that 'the American citizen defends the union, because in defending it he
defends the prosperity and freedom of his
own district.'* Mr. FREEMAN shows how, if
the Swiss States had not respected their
mutual autonomies, they would have fallen
to pieces long ago ; and how they hold
together inseparably, because each knows
that Federal union means combined strength
and individual independence.† It was the
refusal of local independence which caused
the United States to separate from Great
Britain ; it is the concession of it which has

* *Démocratie*, &c., c. vii. p. 186.
† *Fed. Gov.*, p. 121.

made Australia, Canada, and New Zealand loyal colonies to the Crown. Thus Norway has been bound to Sweden, and Hungary to Austria, and the Channel Islands have been attached to Great Britain. Considering such examples, we perceive the force of FORSTER's prediction that the unsuitable centralization of 1800 might lead to disruption of the two countries, and of GRATTAN's eloquent warning, that in destroying the Irish Parliament, PITT had destroyed 'a pillar of the Empire.'

It thus appears that the concession of domestic autonomy to Ireland (1) would leave absolutely intact all the physical force which at present resists separation, and (2) would be likely immensely to increase the moral force which resists it.

But how would the concession of domestic autonomy affect the forces which tend to separation? I submit it would almost annihilate them. These forces are two-fold: emigration and disaffection. As to emigration, its chief cause is want of remunerative employment at home. The Irish seldom like to leave ' the old sod.' But if the internal

affairs of Ireland, instead of being either
wholly neglected or attended to in a hap-
hazard way by very busy strangers who know
very little about them, and have more pressing matters of their own to look after, were
attended to by people who know all about
them, who would have scarcely any other
public interests to attend to, and whose personal interest would be concerned in attending to them well and wisely, we might expect
the encouragement of industry, the development of resources, and the growing prosperity
which, as a matter of fact, nearly always attend self-government elsewhere, and which
constitute the only real check to emigration.
As to Irish disaffection, any child can tell
that it can only be cured by removing its
cause, and that its cause is the persistent disregard of the instinct of nationality, which is
now, and ever has been, the deepest in the
Irish heart. You may do many things for
Ireland, but be well assured you will never
remove disaffection while this cankering
wrong remains. If, however, it were removed, there would be no cause, not even

a plausible excuse, for desire to separate. What influential section of Irishmen could then be supposed to desire it? Not the landlords : their tendencies are the other way. Not the farmers : they know who buy their produce. Not the commercial classes : they would not sever their best business connections. Not the clergy : they have steadfastly resisted separatist theories. Not the people : they are kindly enough in the main, and do not keep up quarrels after the cause of quarrel has passed away. Some fools might propose mischief, but on the whole the Irish are not fools; they know their own interests as well as most people ; and it is clear to every man of common sense that it is the interest of both Islands to pull together.

The tendency of domestic autonomy, therefore, would be to strengthen the force which resists separation, and to weaken the forces which propel towards it.

Now, how would these several forces be affected by the persistent refusal to Irishmen of control of their domestic affairs?

As to the physical force which resists

separation, such refusal would not increase it by a man, or a gun, or a ship, or a shilling. As to the moral force which resists separation, such refusal could not possibly increase it, and would probably diminish it, inasmuch as even the best friends of Great Britain feel that it is really indefensible to refuse a community like Ireland the self-government which is granted to Canada, to New Zealand, and to the Isle of Man. As to emigration, it could not in any way tend to retard and it would probably augment it. As to disaffection, it is hard to anticipate to what extent this may grow if Great Britain persist in refusing the Irish community that control over their own special affairs ' without which,' as Sir GEORGE GREY says, ' no civilised community can be either contented or prosperous.'

Balancing one danger against the other, it appears that the concession of domestic autonomy (1) would not diminish the physical force which resists separation, (2) would strengthen the moral force which resists it, and would diminish, if not entirely remove, (3) the emigration caused by want of home-

employment, and (4) the disaffection produced by disregard of Irish national instincts
and the reasonable wishes of an old, distinct,
and important community. On the other
hand, the refusal of domestic autonomy (1)
would add nothing to the physical force
which resists separation, (2) would diminish
the moral force which resists it, would (3)
stimulate emigration, and would (4) tend to
aggravate disaffection, the two sources from
whence danger of separation arises. I submit, therefore, that it is not the proposal
under consideration which is a delusion, but
the objection to it. If no interests were
concerned but those of Great Britain, these
interests alone would point to the equit-
able adjustment of the relations between
the two Islands on the plan which political
philosophy points out as the appropriate
one, and which, under similar circumstances,
most civilised communities have adopted. If
instead of being a friend I were an enemy
of Great Britain, I would oppose the Home-
Government proposal. If I desired separation, I might be disposed to keep alive

the feud which alone renders separation possible.

But Englishmen, it may be said, are the best judges of their own interests. Be it so. To their judgment, then, let appeal be made; but not to their passion or their prejudice. For many a year their passion and their prejudice upheld the penal laws as necessary to the Empire : their judgment repealed them. For many a year their passion and prejudice upheld the abuses of Church Establishment and agricultural insecurity : their judgment removed them. Just now the last of the dreary old series of abuses is upheld with the dreary old British obstinacy : let British common sense again come to the rescue. Justice counts for much with Englishmen; but if even justice were forgotten, self-interest would point out that if Great Britain is to be safe a reasonable 'modus vivendi' with Ireland must be devised; that persistence in the present system is to play into the hands of the worst enemies of Great Britain and of the Empire; and that when the day of peril comes, as come it must to all, the hand of a brother will be better than the service of a slave.

Objection II.

In considering the last objection you left out of view the contingency of foreign war, and the differences which would be likely to arise between the two Islands on most questions of foreign policy. Ireland is Catholic and Ultramontane: Great Britain is Protestant and Liberal. Ireland loves France: England loves Germany. Ireland loves the Pope: England sympathises with Victor Emmanuel: Ireland loves the United States: England does not so much love them. If the Federal arrangement had existed last year, Ireland would have sent a brigade to the service of France, while Great Britain, if she interfered at all, would have interfered for Germany. Between countries so different in views and tendencies Federal union is impossible.

Answer.

This argument proves too much. If it were true that the two Islands had no interests or sympathies in common, 'the true solvent' would be neither centralization nor Federalism, but—separation. The fact, however, is that though their views differ about foreign policy, it is their interest to come to some mutual understanding concerning it; otherwise neither of them would have any appreciable weight in foreign policy, or perhaps would be able to maintain their political existence in the world at all. Now it is just such a case that Federalism suits. It submits to a common authority all common interests, while it reserves separate interests to be separately dealt with. Moreover, the objection seems to have been made without advertence to the real nature of the Federal system. Under this system it would be as unlawful and as materially impossible for Ireland to intervene on its own account in a foreign war as it is now. She would not have the right, and she would not have the means. Of course it would be equally impossible for Great Britain to interfere except by the decision of the authority to which both Islands would be subject, and in which both would be proportionally represented. 'Two requisites,' as Mr. FREEMAN teaches, 'constitute a Federal Government. On the one hand, each of the members of the union must be wholly independent in those matters which concern each member only. On the other hand, all must be subject to a common power in those matters which concern the members collectively. Thus each member will fix for itself the laws of its criminal jurisprudence, and even the details of its political constitution; and it will do this not as a matter of concession or privilege from any higher power, but as a matter of absolute right by virtue of its inherent powers as an independent commonwealth. But in all matters which concern the general body, the sovereignty of the several members will cease. Each member is perfectly independent within its own sphere; but there is another sphere in which its separate existence vanishes. It is invested with every right of sovereignty on one class of subjects, but there is another class of subjects on which it is incapable of separate political action. The making of peace and war, the sending and receiving ambassadors, generally all that comes within the department of international law, are reserved wholly to the central power.

Indeed the very existence of the several members of the union is diplomatically unknown to foreign nations, which will never be called on to deal with any powers except the central Government. A Federal union in short forms one state in relation to other powers, but many states as regards its internal administration. . . . . Thus, the City of Megalopolis in old times, the State of New York, or the Canton of Zurich now, has absolutely no separate existence in the face of other powers : it cannot make war or peace, or maintain ambassadors or consuls. The common Federal Government of Achaia, America, or Switzerland, is the only body with which foreign nations can have any intercourse. But the internal laws, the law of real property, the criminal law, the electoral law, may be utterly different at Megalopolis and at Sikyôn, at New York and in Illinois, at Zurich and at Geneva. . . . . The system secures to every member full internal independence, but refuses to any member separate external action.' *

* *Hist. Fed. Govt.*, vol. i. pp. 3, 4, 9, 10.

Objection III.

It must be admitted to be likely that the very existence of a domestic legislature in Ireland would constitute a rallying point for Irish disaffection everywhere, a fulcrum on which the 'party of separation' would set their levers, and an influence perpetually operating against the unity of the Empire.

Answer.

I submit that these apprehensions cannot be accepted as likelihoods ; that, on the contrary, the very existence of a domestic legislature in Ireland would abate disaffection in the only effective way, viz., by removing its only reasonable cause ; that in establishing a satisfactory 'modus vivendi' for the two Islands it would deprive 'the party of separation' (if such there be) of their only real influence, viz., the growing belief that such a 'modus vivendi' is impossible; and that so far from operating against unity, it is the only way of ultimately securing it.

But these are only guesses at both sides. From guesses turn to facts.

As a matter of fact we find that the ope-

ration of the Federal system has been, not
against, but in favour of, unity. Mr. FREEMAN
expressly teaches that, under the circumstances for which it is suited, it is 'emphatically a system of union, and of the strength
which follows union.' State Legislatures are,
in fact, as in GRATTAN's phrase, the 'pillars'
of Empire. Whoever wants to destroy Imperial unity commences by destroying, or
trying to destroy, them. Thus of old the
Romans conquered the Achaian league; thus
in the Middle Age Spain worked, bribed, and
fought for centralization of the Dutch provinces; thus in Switzerland the *Internationale* seeks centralization, and labours
against home rule. If the State Legislatures
of America were destroyed, how long would
the American Union stand? If the British
Colonies were denied the management of
their own internal affairs, how long would
they remain attached to the British Empire?
What reason is there to believe that domestic
autonomy on the Federal plan would operate
differently in Ireland from the way in which
it has operated everywhere else?

Still there is risk that it *may* so operate. True. But even if it did, there would operate against it all the material power which now maintains unity, *plus* the vastly increased moral power, which being indisputably in the right would give ; and such paulo-post future risk counts for little as compared with the grave actual dangers of driving a community to desperation by refusing its just rights and ancient liberties, of crowding all sorts of legislative and administrative work on an assembly which has neither time nor local knowledge to deal with them, and of persisting in a system of centralization which the canons of political philosophy, and the experience of the world, show to be unsuitable as an adjustment of the relations between communities possessing common interests, but distinct rights and different internal characteristics.

Objection IV.

But is it not dreadful to break up one of the great capital institutions of the country?

Answer.

If by this be meant the Imperial Parliament, I must respectfully answer that no one, so far as I know, has proposed to break it up. Certainly not Mr. BUTT or Mr. MAGUIRE, or the HOME GOVERNMENT ASSOCIATION. They, on the contrary, propose to leave the Imperial Parliament exactly as it is; except in so far as its efficiency would be increased, and its working facilitated, by relieving it of a certain portion of business which, properly speaking, is not Imperial business at all, and which it has only at a comparatively recent period taken in hand. The Imperial Parliament keeps itself free of the domestic affairs of the Channel Islands and of the Colonies. It lately disembarrassed itself of the domestic affairs of Canada. It is now proposed to disembarrass it of the internal affairs of Ireland. So far from this additional relief tending to break it up, I submit it is just the one thing necessary to extricate it from the 'dead-lock' at which it has arrived, and enable it to mind its own proper business, English,

Scotch, Colonial, and Imperial, the neglect of which is causing such general complaint and such wide-spreading, deep-reaching confusion. It is sorry comfort (said the President of the Miners' Conference the other day) to the poor down-stricken English miner, as his eyes are closing to all earthly things, to tell him that Parliament has not had time to attend to him.

Objection V.

Why this eternal growl? Of what has Ireland now to complain? We have done everything we could think of for her. Two most laborious Sessions of Parliament were given up to rectifying the inequalities of her condition, and redressing the wrongs of her history. If Ireland wants anything more why doesn't she present an united demand for it? She has her full share of representatives; she has had more than her share of attention; she shall always have justice: what more does she want? It is unreasonable, ungrateful, puerile, to keep up this immemorial complaining.

Answer.

In Chapter IV. I have dealt with this objection. Permit me to add one other consideration. Suppose that France or Germany acquired predominance over Great Britain, and that in some new international arrangement it became the interest of Great Britain to form one Imperial State in conjunction with either or both these countries, and to consent that their common affairs should be managed in one Imperial Assembly, would Englishmen and Scotchmen be satisfied that the affairs which were *not* common, the domestic affairs, of their country, should be transacted at Paris or Berlin? They might have power to send a contingent of representatives to such foreign assembly; that contingent, though divided by the necessities of English and Scotch party life, and though generally neutralised and outnumbered, might nevertheless sometimes turn the scales of foreign party contests, and might have some influence over British domestic interests; they might 'chaffer with successive Ministers, and buy concessions at one time with votes given at another time;' the French or German Government for the time being might be animated by the most kindly dispositions towards Great Britain; its leader might be a man of the gentlest heart, and the largest intellect, and the noblest impulses, and the most persuasive eloquence; such a leader might have studied British domestic affairs with earnest rectitude, and rendered Great Britain solid, timely, and generous services; it might be true that if all the British representatives agreed on any demand such united demand would receive the best consideration from the kindly foreign Parliament and the friendly foreign Minister: what Englishman or Scotchman who was not a sneak, with the soul of a slave, would be 'content' with all this? Surely the hearts of Englishmen would say then what the hearts of Irishmen say now: We want to be free to manage our own affairs; self-government does not consist in deputing a contingent of representatives to a foreign legislative assembly; this unanimity which you require from our representatives is impracticable ; even if it were practicable ' united demands ' and foreign concessions do not constitute self-government.   How can we be ' content ' while our domestic affairs are in utter confusion, and while we are refused the liberty to manage them, without which no civilised community was ever yet contented or prosperous?

Objection VI.

The last answer discloses the fallacy of the whole case. The Imperial Parliament is *not* the Parliament of a country ' foreign ' to Ireland. Ireland has no claim to individual national existence. Great Britain conquered her several ages ago ; and she must take the consequences of conquest. During the historical period, at least, Ireland never was a separate nation. She is not a separate nation now, and cannot be treated as such without doing violence to facts. For six hundred years she has been an integral part of the British Empire. There is no difference between a demand of Home Rule for Ireland

and a demand of Home Rule for Cornwall or Wessex. The demand is, therefore, preposterous and untenable.

Answer.

In some senses it is true that Great Britain is not a country ' foreign ' to Ireland. Common interests, neighbouring position, old associations, like races, the same language and literature, close and constant intercourse : all these create that ' certain degree of community' which, in the words of Mr. FREEMAN's canon, ' enable them both to work together up to a certain point.' This ' degree of community,' so far from militating against the Federal theory, is one of the two bases on which it rests, and without which it would be inapplicable. The question is whether there is ' that perfect degree of community, or rather identity,' which would allow them to be ' fused together for all purposes, and to which Federalism is equally inappropriate ;' in other words, whether, as a matter of fact, Ireland stands in the same relation to Great

Britain as one of the English counties, or anything substantially like that relation.

'Perfect identity' between two countries, so that one may be taken as a county of the other, must consist of one or more of the following elements : geographical identity, historical identity, identity of character, identity of condition. Which of these elements of identity exist between Ireland and Great Britain ?

Not geographical identity. Nature marked out Ireland as a distinct country, and set many miles of stormy sea between it and the neighbouring island.

Not historical identity. You could scarcely name two countries lying side by side whose history has been so different.

Not identity of character. There are the most striking, and the most apparently unalterable moral differences between the populations of both countries.

Not identity of condition. Their respective conditions are utterly unlike. One is rich : the other poor. One is a manufacturing country ; the other is an agricultural country.

One has vast mineral wealth; the other has not. One is in the acmé, if not the decline, of prosperity, the other is a 'beginner in the world.' Their territorial systems are different. Their prevailing religions are different. Their statistics can be compared only by contrast.

How, then, can it be said that 'perfect identity' exists? In what sense is it true that one has been 'fused' into a county of the other? Would such an idea occur to any one except in the ardour of disputation? I think not.

As to the argument that Ireland, being conquered by Great Britain, must take the consequences of conquest, if it be worth anything it goes to justify a brute-force government of one community by another, which all political writers declare to be an evil, and which in this case is expressly repudiated on all sides. But in what sense is it true that Great Britain conquered Ireland? Saxons and Normans came over here in vast numbers and incessantly for centuries. After the longest strife in history, they made good their ground and effected a compromise with the

Celtic population, in which the latter got the worst of the bargain. It may be doubtful whether the Celtic races were conquered; but there is no doubt that the incoming races were *not* conquered. These were the conquerors, if any conquest there were. Their blood is in all our veins. Both races have been fused long ago. There is scarcely an Irishman of Celtic name, a MAGUIRE, or an O'DONOGHUE, or a SULLIVAN, without some Saxon or Norman lineage; scarcely a BUTT, or a MARTIN, a SMITH, a SHAW, or a DAUNT, whose Saxon or Norman blood has not had a Celtic intermingling. All are in birth, in race, and in feeling, Irishmen; and to speak of them as descendants of people conquered by Great Britain betrays confusion of thought and inaccuracy of language, not to speak of its being a revival of reminiscences which had better be let die.

As to the statement that during the historical period, at least, Ireland was never a separate nation, I submit that it is neither correct as a fact nor apposite as an argument. In the first place, Ireland was certainly a separate nation during the fifth, sixth, seventh, eighth, ninth, tenth, and eleventh centuries, and these centuries are certainly within the historical period. Again, no one proposes to make Ireland a separate nation now: on the contrary, it is proposed that both Islands shall *not* be separated, and shall remain in strict Federal union. As Mr. MAGUIRE points out, ' No two things could be more opposed in meaning, purpose, and object than Separation and Federalism, that which severs and that which unites.' Lastly, it is in nowise necessary to show that the two countries continued to be separate nations in order to justify the Federal proposal: on the contrary, if they had continued separate Federalism would not be applicable at all.

The objection that for six hundred years Ireland has been an integral part of the Empire appears to me to betray a similar looseness of thought. In the first place, the advocates of the present proposal do not suggest any infraction whatever of the integrity of the Empire. In the second place, the objection implies that which they contend for, namely, that the integrity of the Empire is consistent with the existence of an Irish Parliament, seeing that for the greater part of the six hundred years in question the Irish Parliament was in active existence. If, as a matter of fact, an Irish Parliament was for several hundreds of years compatible with the integrity of the Empire, what becomes of the theory that it is essentially incompatible with it?

But it may be said that the Irish Parliament was a sham, and only registered the decrees of its sister assembly. History does not ratify this allegation. On the contrary, there is nothing clearer than that, though the English Parliament from time to time claimed jurisdiction over the local affairs of Ireland, the Irish Parliament struggled against such claims, and sometimes successfully, sometimes unsuccessfully, but always pertinaciously, asserted its independence. In its earlier days the English Parliament did not interfere at all in domestic affairs. One of its first interferences occurred in the

tenth year of Henry IV.* This interference
was corrected by the Irish Act of that year
enacting that no law should have any force
in Ireland unless made by the Parliament of
Ireland. The same thing occurred in the
tenth year of Henry V., and again in the
twenty-ninth year of Henry VI. In the
time of Richard III. the English Court of
Queen's Bench decided in words quoted
by Lord Coke : 'Hibernia habet Parliamen-
tum et facit leges et nostra statuta non
ligant eam.' In the tenth year of Henry
VII. the English Parliament passed Poyn-
ings' law, partially altering this assumption
and requiring all Irish statutes to be con-
firmed by the King and Council in England.
But in the following reign the Irish Parliament declared, in an address to the Crown,
that 'this realm is free from subjection to
any man's laws, but such as have been
devised and ordained in this realm.' The
same right was again statutably asserted in
1641. In 1689 it was statutably reasserted

* This part of the subject will be found eloquently and
learnedly discussed in a letter to the Drogheda Conference by
Mr. O'Neill Daunt, the author of *Ireland and its Agitators*, &c.

as a protest against an order of the English
Peers, and was defended in the famous
pamphlets of Lucas, Molyneux, and Swift.
In 1719, when Ireland was utterly prostrate,
the English Parliament passed an Act in the
contrary sense,* but in 1782 the Irish Parliament adopted the celebrated Declaration
of Right ' that by our fundamental laws the
subjects of this realm cannot be bound by any
legislation save by the King, Lords, and
Commons of Ireland.' The English Parliament statutably ratified this right; and
the question was declared to be settled for
ever.† On this basis matters continued until
the Union, when the settlement was reversed,
a new settlement effected with an amount of
fraud and violence that would legally vitiate
any contract between individuals, and legislation based on what even Charles James
Fox declared to be ' the false and abomi-
nable presumption that the English could
legislate better for the Irish than they could
do for themselves—a presumption founded
on the most arrogant tyranny.'‡ From that

---

* 6 Geo. I. C. 5.   † 21 and 22 Geo. III. C. 47.
‡ Address to the Whig Club, A.D. 1800.

day to this the restoration of Irish legislative independence has been the dream of the Irish national heart, and the aspiration of nearly every generous Irish spirit. The desire of it was the latent force behind every agitation. Its refusal was the cause of, though not a justification for, every rebellion. For this TONE plotted and EMMETT died. It gave the key-note to some of MOORE's best lyrics. It underlay the Emancipation struggle and outlived its success. It rallied the millions under O'CONNELL in 1843. It caused the desperation of 1848. It dictated the Limerick Declaration of 1867.* It is now just the one point on which the best educated thought and the deepest popular sympathy in Ireland coincide.

We may, or may not, accept Mr. MILL's teaching, that ' where the sentiment of nationality exists in any force, there is a prima facie case for uniting all the members of the nation-

---

* This document produced a sensation when it appeared, and is worth studying now. It was published by Mr. Fowler, Dublin. It was signed by twelve hundred priests at the instance of the eloquent and patriotic Dean O'BRIEN of Limerick, a man to whom Ireland owes much.

ality under the same Government;'* but
every fair disputant will, I think, admit that
there *is* a difference between the demand of
domestic autonomy by such a community, so
divided geographically, so distinct historically,
so different actually, so steadfast in national
aspiration, and such a demand if made by
Cornwall or Wessex, and that to base one's
objection to the Home Government proposal
on the supposition that Ireland is in the
relation to Great Britain of an English
county is to put it on a basis which will not
stand the test of critical examination.

Objection VII.

To this line of argument there is one con-
clusive objection, and it might be stated in
one word, viz., Scotland. Here is an instance
of a country geographically distinguished from
England, historically distinct, differing from
England in character, in religion, in race, in
territorial system, in likings and dislikings,
a country of which the bravest inhabitants
hated England traditionally, and made war
upon her periodically, an ancient, gallant

* *Representative Government*, p. 120.

nation, whose kings held their own for a thousand years, and at last went to reign over England herself. According to the principles laid down in the preceding pages, this was a case for self-government if ever such a case could be said unmistakeably to exist. Yet while Scotland was self-governed she was poor, barbarous, and disturbed. Since she gave up self-government, she became rich, civilised, and peaceful. In the name of common sense let Ireland follow this wise example. Let her stop talking and fall to work. Let her give up 'nationality,' till her fields, develop her manufactures, and mind her business. Instead of 'Erin-go-bragh,' let her (as SYDNEY SMITH advised long ago) cry, 'Erin-go-bread-and-cheese!'

Answer.

This sounds very well ; we have heard it a hundred times, and are doomed to hear it a thousand times again ; but as an objection to the Federal proposal it does not bear examination.

In the first place, Scotland has not as strong a case for autonomy as Ireland. Scotland and England constitute one island ? Ireland constitutes another. ' Our patent to be a state, not a shire,' said Master GOOLD in 1799, ' came from Heaven.' The history of Scotland, though distinct from that of England, is parallel to it. The religious systems of England and Scotland, though differing in details, are in principle identical. So with their territorial systems. So with their social systems.

But though the Scotch case for autonomy is not as strong as that of Ireland, it is of considerable strength, and it seems obvious that some fallacy must lurk in the line of an argument which leads to the extraordinary position that because the Scotch are industrious, shrewd, and energetic—they are not to be trusted with the management of their own legislative and administrative affairs !

All political thinkers concur in admitting and asserting that, as a rule, civilised communities thrive best when they have the management of their own affairs. Suppose it were established that Scotland is an exception to this rule, what then ? The exception only proves the rule. To draw a general conclusion from a particular case is a fallacy indeed.

But is the prosperity of Scotland due to the abnegation of her autonomy? There is nothing whatever to show it. Reduced to logical formula the argument would stand thus : Scotland gave up self-government ; she prospered ; therefore her prosperity is owing to her having given up self-government. It might as well be argued that inasmuch as ROBERT BURNS took to toddy, and became a great poet, he became a great poet because he took to toddy.

So far from this argument being sound, it is possible, (to say the least,) that Scotland prospered, not because she surrendered her self-government, but despite of her having partially done so. Political constitutions count for much ; but they do not count for everything. Communities, like individuals, often thrive under adverse circumstances. Lord MACAULAY shows how the desire of each man to better himself and the constant advances of physical science will produce an important improvement in the condition of a nation despite great political drawbacks, or even great national calamities ; and ROBERT RAMSEY wrote an able tract to prove that the loss of Scotch legislative independence was the real hindrance which Scotch industry and energy has had to overcome.*

The really weighty consideration, however, is that the whole objection happens to be founded on an inaccurate statement of the fact. It assumes that Scotland is not to a great extent virtually self-governed, or rather that it has only the same amount of control over its own affairs that Ireland possesses. But every politician and every well-informed man knows that the contrary is the case. Scotland is, and for a hundred years has been, to a large extent virtually self-governed, while Ireland, for seventy years at least, has been virtually ruled by Great Britain. Every one has heard of the sort of supplemental 'Scotch Parliament,' in which Scotch members have almost as much of their own way at West-

---

* See *Scotland interested in the Question of Federal Parliaments.* By Robert Ramsey. Leckie, Glasgow.

minster as if they sat in the old Hall at Edinburgh : Irish members have no such privilege. Nearly every important Scotch administrative office is held by a Scotchman : in Ireland an Irishman is rarely intrusted with any really important administrative office. Most of the great Scotch proprietors reside for the greater part of the year on their own estates : most of the great Irish pro- prietors are absentees. Royalty spends half the year in Scotland : its visits to Ireland are rare indeed. Irish nationality is held to be treasonable, is snubbed, caricatured, and set at defiance : to sing an Irish national song in the streets of an Irish city is a very perilous proceeding : Scotch nationality has been conciliated with the wisest care ; so that the very garb and the very banners, the very instruments, and the very music with which for centuries hereditary foes and gallant rebels charged the English lines, now hold the most honoured places in the army of Great Britain. England's dealings with both countries can be compared only by contrast. Under the forms of a centralised Government Scotland happily possesses most of the realities of self-government. Though they gave up the name, our canny neighbours kept a large share of the thing.

But, it may be said, why not, without disturbing the present legislative arrangements, so far modify them, practically, as to give Ireland the same advantages that Scotland possesses? Several reasons forbid this. The Scotch members themselves are beginning to grumble at the arrangement. Scotch business has latterly been delayed, neglected, or hurried through; and many Scotchmen think that their local business would be done better as well as more expeditiously if their representatives met together in the old Hall in Parliament Square at Edinburgh. Dr. BEGG, an eminent Scotch Presbyterian Minister, said the other day at Edinburgh that one single year of Scotch law-making would do more to promote the material interests of Scotland and elevate her social condition than a hundred years of legislation for Scotland in Westminster. Moreover, the arrangement at best is a highly artificial one, and the conditions which render it practicable in Scotland do not exist in Ireland. Amongst Irish representatives the two great parties are nearly balanced; amongst Scotch representatives all but a small minority belong to one party. Political affairs may settle themselves into peculiar adjustments to suit certain exigencies, but the attempt to apply such peculiar adjustments to different circumstances nearly always ends in disappointment and disaster. The rule is a safer guide than the exception.

As to the general exhortations to mind our own business, they are excellent in themselves. They would be more likely to be successful if they were not quite so supercilious. But as an objection to the Home Government proposal they have no relevancy. It is precisely our own business which we propose to mind—a business which in the hands of others has been admittedly neglected and mismanaged.

Objection VIII.

One of the last observations suggests the real difficulty of the case. The truth is that Ireland does not possess the conditions which

render self-government safe. It is not one
community : it consists of two communities.
The northern Protestants and the southern
Catholics are as different as if they lived a
thousand miles apart ; except that, being near
each other, they ' hate each other with a truly
neighbourly hatred.' Give Ireland autonomy
and these two communities will be at each
other's throats in a month. Her worst enemy
could not bestow on Ireland a more fatal
gift than that for which some Irishmen are
now blindly seeking.

Answer.

I submit that this objection, like the preceding one, is based on an exaggerated statement of the fact. Mr. DISRAELI's famous
novel taught us that in a certain restricted
and artificial sense there are in England itself
' two nations ; ' another eminent statesman-
novelist reveals Normans and Saxons in
English daily life ; but, except in some such
restricted and archaic sense, it cannot be said
that Ireland consists of ' two communities.'
The differences are not at all as great as the
objection implies, and they are daily dimi-

nishing. The Celtic, Saxon, and Norman
races are in reality almost as much fused in
Ireland as they are in Great Britain. They
are inextricably mingled together in all social, commercial, and neighbourly relations
throughout the country; nay, as we have
seen, they are actually intermingled in the
lineage and the blood of most Irishmen.
As to difference in religion, it exists in Ireland as it exists in nearly all civilised countries; but, as in nearly all civilised countries,
it is agreed that such differences shall be
reciprocally conceded, and that he best
honours his own religion who most practically shows that its outcomes are charity,
self-control, and consideration for the rights,
feelings, and liberties of others. ' Sweetness
and light' are, indeed, sometimes wanting in
public utterances at both sides; but it is
notorious that such uncharitable utterances
cause most pain, as of course they do most
damage, to the side from whence they proceed, and that they are practically repudiated
by the good sense and good feeling of nearly
everyone concerned. On the other hand,
even the most casual observer cannot fail to

be struck with the fairness, the courtesy, and the conciliatory tone of most men of real mark in both communions. Nor is this conciliatory disposition a matter of words only; it is far more remarkably evidenced by facts. In ' Protestant Ulster' Catholics are rapidly increasing in numbers and rising in wealth and station. In ' Catholic Munster' Protestants are elected by Catholic votes to parliamentary and municipal honours; and Protestant traders enjoy the larger share of Catholic custom. The fact is that, speaking generally, and excepting certain well-meaning but cross-grained individuals, and certain hot little localities, differences of religion are scarcely considered at all in giving a vote or in buying an article, in selecting an assist-ant or in making a friend. The objection under discussion is therefore based on an inaccurate and exaggerated statement of the facts.

Moreover, it is clearly open to the re-joinder that it ' proves too much.' The ex-istence of different religions and different races in a community, or even a considerable degree of active antagonism between them, does not incapacitate from self-government. If it did, the greatest nations of modern times should be considered thus incapacitated, and nearly every civilised community should beg some barbarous one to take charge of it, in order to keep it from laying violent hands on itself.

So far is this from being the case, it may be safely stated that civil freedom is one of the great reconcilers of civil differences. A graceful Greek legend tells how foes were made friends by being sent to 'pull together' in the same boat. Everybody knows what little good comes of interference between man and wife. If the experience of the world counts for anything, it is better, in civilised communities at least, 'to let forces balance themselves,' rather than 'by importation of foreign make-weights throw them more thoroughly out of gear.'*

Nevertheless, it is not only right, but most salutary and important, to remember that, whether Ireland remain centralized or obtain its autonomy, this objection points to a real danger. There is no magic in any political

* See *Contemporary Review*, vol. vi. p. 185.

system, and no hope for any mixed community under any conceivable system, unless its
citizens have the common sense to 'agree to
differ.' Let him who fosters hate, and feeds
the flame of ancient feud between Irishmen,
be well assured that, whether he knows it or
not, whether he gives way to sudden passion
or follows the bad custom of traditional
bigotry, whether he expresses himself in the
rough epithets of the mob or in the dainty
phrase of elegant scholarship, he is in reality
doing the work of the worst enemies of
Ireland, and making himself an apostle of
primeval barbarism ; he is doing one man's
part to stop progress and prevent prosperity,
to dishonour religion and degrade manhood,
to make life wretched, and liberty, under any
form of government, impossible.

Objection IX.

To such arguments able and kindly Englishmen answer in effect, We cannot deny
that there is a strong theoretical case for a
Federal adjustment of the relations of Great
Britain and Ireland ; we must admit that,
were we in your place, we would seek such

an adjustment; we would not 'stand' having anybody domineer over our own domestic affairs. But then—Irishmen are not Englishmen. To be candid; you, Irishmen, are not fit to be intrusted with the management of your own affairs. Owing to a series of unfortunate circumstances, and of great errors at both sides, your country is still in 'a sad mess.' Your political education is, as yet, utterly imperfect. Freedom requires self-control; you have none. Freedom requires knowledge; you prefer dreams. You labour under an unfortunate instability of thought, a craving for excitement, an abhorrence of work, a chronic restlessness, that are incompatible with successful self-government. Look at your corporations, what neglect of business! what jobbery! what waste of time in talk! Do you really wish your country to be governed as your cities are governed? Look at your parliamentary elections, what violence! what 'bosh!' what time-serving! what electors! what candidates! Do you not see that your country would drift to ruin, if left at the mercy of such people?

Answer.

If good round abuse, incessant lecturing, and a candour disembarrassed of any regard for our feelings, be services to any community, we ought to be very grateful. We 'catch it' nearly every day, and sometimes a dozen times a day. Language has no phrase of scorn too hard for us, wit no arrow too sharp for us. If half that is said of us were true, and were the whole truth, we certainly ought to be 'cognosced,' as the Scotch call the transfer of the affairs of lunatics to fit guardianship.

This, however, is only one view of our character. Kindlier writers and speakers, and writers and speakers in kindlier moods, almost reverse the picture, and in their generous appreciation and their gracious compliments, fall into a strain which sober-minded people must ruefully confess to be almost as unreal and one-sided as the other.

This contrast of English views has its counterpart in Irish social life. Some Irishmen are quite proud of self-abasement, quite exultant in self-accusation, ''umble' as URIAH HEEP; disposed as TROTTY VECK to whine, ' We are bad, bad—born bad ! ' Others glorify our virtues, exalt our powers, and ignore our faults beyond all bounds of reason.

Where does the truth lie ? Pretty much where it nearly always lies—between the extremes.

The truth is, that we are not much better or much worse than other people ; and this truth refutes the objection under consideration.

Observe that in order to make a case for depriving a nation of the control of its own affairs, just as in order to make a case for depriving a man of the control of his own affairs, a special incapacity to manage them must be proved, and the onus of proof lies on those who assert such special incapacity.

Now I submit that in the case of Ireland there are absolutely no proofs of such special incapacity.

The only proofs alleged are the mismanagement of our corporations, and the violence and time-serving of our elections. So far as these exist they are to be regretted; but their extent is exaggerated. Though our corporations are not models, they are at least up to the average of such bodies elsewhere, and are far better than many such bodies in the most famous of self-governed communities. No Irish city is so badly governed as London itself. The British vestry has no Irish rival in general incapacity. Who suggests that Englishmen are, therefore, incapable of self-government? Irish elections are, indeed, susceptible of improvement; but they are not worse than English elections. Kidderminster is, at least, a match for Sligo. The 'lambs' of Birmingham exceed the Tipperary boys in violence as much as they are inferior to them in fun, and in that love of country which (unless the observer's head be broken,) almost redeems the violence. As to Irish representatives, it seems to be admitted that the average Irish member is equal to the average English or Scotch member. Of members above the average, the Imperial Legislature contains few better administrators than Mr. FORTESCUE, Mr. MONSELL, and Lord DUFFERIN;

few better debaters than Lord O'HAGAN, Mr.
MAGUIRE, Mr. DOWSE, Mr. PLUNKET, and Dr.
BALL.

But while Irishmen have shown at least
average capacity for legislative and administrative freedom at home, they have shown
more than the average of such aptitude
abroad. Not to speak of the past, we have
quite recently seen Irishmen govern Australia,
New Zealand, Canada, India, and several of
the United States, and the descendants of
Irishmen govern Algeria, Spain, and Austria.
In these governments they have shown, says
the calm and philosophical *Spectator*, 'an
aptitude for government of the hard, personal, practical kind,' the very aptitude
which it is supposed Irishmen never possess.
'Whether D'ARCY McGEE or General SHERI-
DAN, or Mr. DUFFY, the Irishman abroad is
a stern, clear man . . . inventive, resource-
ful, far-seeing, and brave.' 'An Irish civil
service,' continues the *Spectator*, 'composed
of such men, picked for the work, trained for
it, and encouraged to be independent, would
govern the country as it has never been

governed yet, with a force, directness, and
honesty which in a few years would suppress
all opposition, and make the law what it has
become under more difficult circumstances in
India, the final arbiter. This, we may rely
on it, is the only kind of government which
suits the national genius, and the only one
which in Ireland will ever reconcile freedom
with order.' 'These people,' says Sir GEORGE
GREY, 'possess the faculties of legislation and
administration in an equal degree with any
other nation on earth. They are the people
who, removed to a new sphere, in the colonies
or elsewhere, where fair scope is given to
their talents, have yielded many men who
have governed the outlying portions of the
Empire with dignity and success, who have
produced from their own body ministers and
legislators who have devised, framed, and
passed laws which Great Britain herself is
beginning to copy.' *

If to these considerations we add that, as
'nothing succeeds like success, so nothing
fosters qualities which fit for freedom so much

* Tract on the *Land Question*, p. 12.

as freedom itself, and that too long continued 'leading strings' are as injurious for a community as for a man. I trust that the most impartial enquirer will have no difficulty in considering, at least, as 'not proven' the allegation that the Irish community is below the average of civilised communities, and unfit to be intrusted with the management of even its own domestic affairs.

Objection X.

Irish Protestants sometimes say : In principle we are with you. The desirableness of self-government is almost too plain for argument; it is certain that Ireland is not self-governed; it is admitted that those who undertake to manage our affairs have mismanaged them ; the theoretical fitness of the Federal adjustment is obvious; there is in principle no reason, (as shrewd and genial old CHARLES LEVER said the other day in *Blackwood,*) why Irishmen should be obliged to swell the ranks of English parties before being permitted to mind Irish business. Moreover, we Protestants do not love subjection or despise civil freedom; it is not our way. We love old Ireland as much as any 'wearer of the green.' We desire her independence as sincerely as our fathers did when they achieved it in 1782. Nevertheless it is impossible for us to join the Home Government movement. The reason is this. In every free representative government the majority rule; in Ireland the majority are Roman Catholics : hence, if Ireland had free representative government, it would be ruled by Roman Catholics. The project under discussion is a Roman Catholic project, and its success would result in Roman Catholic ascendency. We wish our Roman Catholic fellow countrymen well, but they must excuse us from putting our necks under their feet.

Answer.

This objection demands the most respectful consideration, especially as Rev. Dr. LANG-LEY, in a recent able pamphlet, assures us that but for it 'every branch of the Reformed Church would vote for Home Rule.'* For

* *The Irish Crisis.* Hodges, Dublin : p. 19.

clearness' sake let us take separately the two reasons on which it rests, viz., that the present is a Roman Catholic project, and that it would lead to Roman Catholic ascendency.

The project, in its inception, is certainly not Roman Catholic. It is as Protestant in its origin as the movement of 1782. Protestants are its chief leaders, and have its chief direction. It is notorious that the Catholic Episcopacy has not as yet approved of it. Moreover, the Association has declared the repudiation of Religious Ascendency to be one of its fundamental rules, and it prints this repudiation on every card of membership. Mr. BUTT goes so far as to suggest that any question involving such ascendency should be placed out of the jurisdiction of the Irish Parliament. In fact, there is no conceivable sense in which it is true that the project, quâ project, is Roman Catholic.

As to its success resulting in Roman Catholic ascendency, I submit that the syllogism above stated fails by its first premiss. It is not true that in a free representative government the majority rides down the

minority. No politico-philosophic authority
warrants such an assumption. On the contrary, such an assumption is diametrically
opposed to the first principles of representative
government. It is of the very essence of
civil liberty that the majority should *not* ride
down the minority. It is the very pride of
representative government that the rights of
minorities are protected. It is the very glory
of political philosophy to make intelligence,
education, and property, of more weight in
social affairs than mere ' count of heads.' If
this assumption were true, all civilised communities would be debarred from representative institutions, because in all civilised
communities religious opinions differ in un-
equal proportions.

But it may be rejoined that this is only
when things go right : what if they go wrong ?
In this world anything may go wrong ; and
any political institution may be abused. The
going wrong in this case is a danger to be
guarded against. But is it a danger for Irish
Protestants to tremble at ? Like other people,
Irish Protestants have their faults ; but we

have yet to learn that a tendency to tremble is amongst these faults. I submit that if ever there were a case in which men of sense and spirit might be relieved from reasonable apprehension, this is one. Counting nearly a third of the whole Irish community, possessed of nine-tenths of its territorial wealth, dowered with nearly all its aristocratic rank, having had a long 'start' of their fellow-countrymen in every profession, in every trade, in the whole race of life, possessed of the thousand advantages which grow out of assured position and ancestral wealth and traditional culture and hereditary refinement—for such a body to tremble at taking the common risks of free citizenship would be strange indeed. I know my Protestant fellow-countrymen too well to believe that, when the issue is fairly put, they will take the inglorious alternative, and nervously renounce the rights of free citizens in order to cling to the skirts of an alien dominancy which their fathers rejected nearly a hundred years ago. Rather, I believe, they will put to themselves Dr. LANG-LEY's shrewd question : 'Are the interests of

Irish Protestants so dear to England as we suppose them to be?' and give the right answer to the 'query' which the most illustrious thinker who ever wore their lawn addressed to all his fellow-citizens :—' Do you not inhabit the same spot of earth, breathe the same air, and live under the same Government? Why, then, should you not conspire in one and the same design to promote the common good of your country?' *

Objection XI.

Some Irish Catholics say : In principle we are with you. The desirableness of self-government for a civilised community is clear. Its desirableness for Ireland is what we have always maintained. Our fathers struggled for it through all fortunes. It is one of the deepest wishes of our own hearts. We are nearly all expressly and personally pledged to it since O'CONNELL's time. Catholicity and Nationality have always been associated in the past ; it would be the worst of all misfortunes to have them disassociated in

* Bishop Berkeley's *Irish Querist*, p. 10.

the future. Nevertheless, we must hold aloof from the HOME GOVERNMENT ASSOCIATION. We don't like it, or its leaders, or its ways. It has raised the question of self-government inopportunely. We were engaged at the Education Question, and had it in fair course of settlement, when the public mind was distracted and the popular force divided by the Home Government proposals. The originators and leaders of the Association are Protestants, and we don't quite trust such originators or leaders ; especially in this instance, when we have reason to suspect that their chief object is to spite Mr. GLADSTONE for having done us justice in the Church and Land Questions. Moreover, its result might be a revival, more or less, of Protestant Ascendency. See how the Catholics are dealt with in some of the Catholic cantons of Switzerland where Protestants have been allowed to take the lead in public affairs. We wish our Protestant fellow-citizens well ; but they must excuse us from playing their little game, and letting them slip back under a new pretext to their old position of political ascendency.

Answer.

This objection also demands the most respectful consideration ; especially as it is
tolerably certain that but for it nearly every
Catholic in Ireland would be for Home Rule.
It turns on three points : (1) the opportuneness of the proposal; (2) its Protestant origin ;
(3) the danger of a revived Protestant political ascendency.

(1.) As to the opportuneness of the proposal : I must admit for myself that I would
have preferred its postponement until the Education Question had been settled. Whatever
concerns the souls of men is of more importance than any temporal concern whatever.
Even as regards political affairs, it is true, as
Mr. MILL expresses it, that 'the worth of any
State is the worth of the individuals compos-
ing it.' If Irish men and women were reared
without faith in God, or hope of heaven, or
charity to man, Irish Nationality would be
worthless and the future of our country dark
indeed.

> Freedom comes from God's right hand,
>   And needs a godly train,
> 'Tis righteous men can make our land
>   A nation once again.

It is, however, one thing to put forward a proposal, quite another thing to deal with it when it has been put forward and has actually 'come to the front' for public discussion and parliamentary settlement. In the practical affairs of life one cannot have everything one's own way; one must only deal with questions as they arise, each on its merits. If the merits of the Home Government proposal be as clear as most Irish Catholics admit them to be, I submit that its opportuneness or inopportuneness is a matter of minor importance. As regards educational interests, I submit that no course could be so injurious as that of creating a factitious antagonism between them and the ancient national instincts of the Irish people. This, in fact, is the very 'game' of those who are antagonists both of Irish self-government and of Irish educational freedom. 'Wait,' they whisper, 'until those interests are set clashing; then you will see "wigs on the green;" and after that there will be no more heard of either of these crotchets.' I submit that there is no reason for such antagonism, and that it would indeed be playing the game of our opponents to create it. Freedom of legislation and freedom of education are two distinct, but not contradictory, proposals ; most Irish Catholics are in favour of both ; no policy could be so bad as that which would tend to render one incompatible with the other. It can be no injury to Irish Catholics that many distinguished and influential Protestant gentlemen are prepared to advocate one of the interests dearest to their hearts, although they do not advocate the other. If ever there were a case for ' agreeing to differ ' this seems to be one.

Moreover, every practical politician knows that, if the Education Question is to be settled in the Imperial Parliament, the likelihood of a settlement in accordance with Irish opinion is indefinitely, though not directly, increased by the imminency of the Home Government proposal ; while, if it is to be settled in an Irish Parliament, Irishmen will have no real difficulty in coming to an understanding with each other about it.

(2.) As to the origin of the Home Government proposal, I submit that a good thing is not rendered bad by Protestants proposing it, and that as to this particular proposal it would never have a chance of success unless the Protestants of Ireland, to a large extent, supported it. That they might one day do so was the hope of some of the noblest hearts Irish Catholicism ever possessed; now that they are disposed to do so shall we coldly turn away from them? Are we to desert our own old flag of nationality because our fellow-countrymen join it? This would be utterly absurd, inconceivably unworthy. Irish Catholics say rather to every

> . . . Irish-born man,
> If you're to Ireland true,
> We heed not race, nor creed, nor clan,
> We've hands and hearts for you.

As to the alleged 'imperfection of motive,' I submit that we must judge others as we claim to be judged ourselves—not by imputed motives, but by words and deeds. As to the government of the Association, if there be any preponderance of Protestant influence, it seems due to those who so generously came forward to assist in the national work, and it

was conferred by the free votes of a constituency more than three-fourths Catholic.
Moreover, the Association is itself only provi-
sional, and in due time will be developed on a
wider basis, when all legitimate influences will
have their due weight in its working and
direction.

(3.) It is, of course, conceivable that, as
happened in some Swiss Cantons and some
Continental States, the Catholic majority
might so far neglect its civic duties, and
abnegate its civic rights, as to allow a Protestant ascendency. But this is not likely to
occur in Ireland. Whatever be the faults of
Irish Catholics, indifference to public interests
and depreciation of civic rights are not
amongst them. It would be puerile for Irish
Catholics to ask Englishmen to govern them,
lest, if Ireland were free, their Protestant fellow-countrymen should get the better of
them.

For both Irish Catholics and Irish Protestants Mr. MAGUIRE's earnest counsel is wise :—
'Be tolerant of each other; make fair allow-
ance for prejudices of birth, class, creed, and

education. Learn to think more of each other than of any other people. You were born on the same soil. You own the same land as your mother. Be proud to make any sacrifice, other than that of principle, to disarm hostility and bring about good feeling. Thus you will lay the foundation of that union which is strength and force and power and success in all lawful undertakings.'

Objection XII.

The true ground of objection to the Federal proposal is not that it is ultra-Catholic or ultra-Protestant, for it evidently is neither, but that it is ultra-revolutionary. Consider the times in which we live and the danger that threatens all civilised society. While we are discussing politico-philosophic niceties and arguing out petty difficulties, THE REVO-LUTION is gaining ground. It is enrolling its thousands in every civilised land. It is preaching its doctrines in all tongues. It has its newspapers in most continental capitals. It threatens India with one hand

and Ireland with the other. It nearly burned Paris. It frightens London. It dominates in Rome. It enlists in its service the prostituted beauty of woman and the prostituted genius of man. It is armed with dagger and torch, and pistol and poison. On its banners are the terrible mottoes : 'Lust is lawful; ' 'Property is robbery ;' 'Assassination is justifiable ;' 'the Bible is an imposture ;' 'the Church is a swindle ;' 'God is a myth.' Fortunately it is, as yet, almost unknown in Ireland. But its latest move is said to be to take advantage of Irish disaffection in order to introduce itself here. Remember that the founder of the *Internationale* is the son of a Cork peasant,* and that it is not long since the *Empire Cluseret* was proposed to be set up in Cork by the redoubtable CLUSERET himself. As I write ' an illustrious member ' of the Society is announced to have taken up his residence in Dublin. In view of such dangers how can you ask us to favour any democratic movement, to loosen the bonds

---

* *Les Mystères de l'Internationale* (Paris: E. Dentu), p. 29 et seq. Quoted in *Dublin Review*, October 1871.

of empire, to attorn to the mob, to make friends with the Fenians? This is rather a time for all who love order, society, civilization, and religion to close their ranks, to resist all democratic tendencies, and to decline to have anything to do with the insurrectionary and the disloyal.

Answer.

I submit that this objection is founded on a misconception both of the state of the case and of the nature of the Federal proposal.

It mistakes the nature of the case in overlooking the fact that the present condition of Ireland constitutes in itself the ' proximate occasion ' for communistic temptations and the choicest ground for communistic conspiracy. It is beneath the shadow of great centralizations that Communism grows. It is on chronic discontent it thrives. Political abuses are its provender. If you be a friend of the Commune, by all means stick up for over-centralization ; resist reform; perpetuate abuse ; let property lean on alien domination : let religion be set at feud with nationality :

let disaffection canker the hearts of the
people; and let the conviction grow in the
minds of the most sober, cool-headed, and
cultivated citizens that Government is making
a mistake, and that the popular discontent is
not without a cause. But if you hate Communism, alter the state of facts which give it
a chance; remove the abuses which may
serve as its fulcrum; let property lean on
right; let religion and nationality go hand-
in-hand; make popular feeling the friend,
not the foe, of the commonwealth: remove discontent by removing its cause; and secure for
Government the honest approval of all capable
and cultivated citizens. There is no service
to order so judicious as that of anticipating
the revolutionary violence which respects no
right, by the wise constitutional development
which permits no wrong.

Again: the objection mistakes the nature
of the Federal proposal in overlooking the
fact that it is conservative rather than
democratic—constructive, not destructive. It
proposes to conserve ancient rights and
local institutions, to restore 'a pillar to the

Empire,' to build a bulwark against revolution. In Switzerland, as we have seen, the Commune labours for centralization, the friends of order for Home Rule. In France the best men of all parties concur in thinking that over-centralization was the great error of the Empire, and in seeking to remedy it by the establishment of departmental councils. In the complicated problem of Austrian (Cisleithan) politics the only thing very clear is that the Conservatives work for Home Rule, the ultra-Radicals for centralization. Everywhere it is well understood by sound politicians that where the conditions for the Federal arrangement exist it is, as Mr. FREEMAN says, 'a source of strength and a bond of union;' that Empires are safest when, as DE TOCQUEVILLE says of the United States, every citizen feels that in defending the Union he is defending the independence and prosperity of his own community, and that it would be as wise for an admiral, before going to battle, to crowd all his guns and concentrate all authority into one ship, as it is for allied communities in a time of danger

to centralize power in one State and leave the
sister communities disorganized, dissatisfied,
and untrained in the habits which grow only
with self-reliance and self-government.

As to the Fenians, they, like all men, are
entitled to justice; and it is the barest justice
to say that we have not a tittle of evidence
identifying them with the atheistical, incen-
diary, predatory, and licentious 'Revolution'
of continental Europe.   On the contrary,
there is every reason to believe that they have
kept themselves clear of it.   The most daring
of them have repudiated it with scorn.   In
truth (as Mr. BUTT well points out*), there is
no people on earth less disposed to ultra
democracy than the Irish.   Their traditional
tendencies and their inmost instincts are all
the other way, and point to respect for rank,
authority, the family and religion.   How sad
to let such instincts be perverted!   How wise
to develop them as only justice and freedom
can!

As to 'attorning to the rabble,' it is a phrase
I repeat with reluctance.   By all means with-

---

* *Federalism*, pp. 64, 102.

stand the people when they are wrong; but what is the sense of withstanding them when they are right? A disposition to despise our fellow-countrymen is not one to be cultivated. Supercilious kid-glove patriotism was never worth much; and it is nearly quite worthless now. We have all smiled at the story of the Munster peasant who, having emigrated to Canada, on being asked how he would vote, answered: Against the Government of course! The aristocratic or dilettante 'irreconcilables,' who are never at ease unless they are opposed to the people, commit a blunder less excusable and more absurd.

As to 'untying the bonds of Empire,' nothing of the sort is proposed. The material securities would remain as they are. The moral ties would be indefinitely strengthened. 'Under an Irish Government we would in seven years become more identified with England than we have in seven centuries of oppression.' *

But can we join a movement in which the disloyal appear to have merged their claims?

* *Federalism, &c.* p. 76.

Certainly. It was the highest aspiration of
the most generous statesmanship that with
the disposition to do justice by constitutional
means confidence in such means might be
restored, and the pursuit of ends compatible
with the constitution renewed. This aspiration has been realised with unexpected rapidity. Is it now proposed to reverse the lesson,
to bid the people be hopeless of the constitution, to convince them that the existence of
the Empire is incompatible with civil liberty,
to teach them that though their rulers can be
stirred to tremendous activity by the merest
prick of insurrection, they are inexorable in
their resistance to constitutional efforts, however enthusiastic, reasonable, or widely supported ?

But this spirit of liberty is dangerous and
liable to perversion ? No doubt. If we would
know what political institutions most tend to
avert the danger and prevent the perversion,
let us hear it taught in the weighty words of
HENRY GRATTAN : ' Do you not put out the
spirit of liberty when you destroy the organ,
constitutional and capacious, through which

that spirit may be safely and discreetly conveyed? What is the excellence of our constitution? Not that it performs prodigies, and prevents the birth of vices which are inseparable from human nature, but that it provides an organ in which those vices may play and evaporate, and through which the humours of society may pass without preying upon the vitals. Parliament is the body where the whole intellect of the country may be collected, and where the spirit of patriotism, of liberty, and of ambition, may act under the control of that intellect, and under the check of publicity and observation. But if once these virtues or defects were forced to act in secret conclave or in dark divan, they would produce, not opposition but, conspiracy.' *

Objection XIII.

What Ireland really wants is not political development, or even social development, but industrial development. For such development capital is necessary. This capital

* Grattan's Speeches, p. 327.

can be expected only from England. Why disassociate yourselves from those whose capital you desire?

Answer.

No such disassociation is proposed. A man is not said to disassociate himself from his neighbour by managing without interference the affairs of his own household. Besides, English capital is wisely cosmopolitan. It invests as readily in Russia as in Canada. It goes freely wherever it is likely to come back with profit. It seeks not political subserviency, but a good investment. Indeed, such subserviency deters rather than attracts it: it rightly considers it ' un-English.' The promised influx of English capital was one of the great arguments for the union : we have waited for it seventy years, and it has not come, or shown any signs of coming. If it ever come it will be because of the conviction that it will be safely and profitably employed. Shrewd men of business button their pockets to West-British ' blarney.' Moreover, it is doubtful whether we want English capital at all. Disaffection to centralized rule and distrust in the knowledge and intentions of their rulers induce our people to hoard in banks and stockings, or take to foreign countries, more than would be required for all our industrial purposes. If we be wise some future historian will tell ' quam cito libertate recuperatâ respublica crevit.'

Objection XIV.

This new agitation is disappointing to English statesmen. It seems to say that the policy of equal justice is insufficient to disarm disaffection. Immediately after the Imperial Parliament has laboured most strenuously to do justice to Ireland it is ungratefully told that it is incompetent to rule Ireland at all. Just as Mr. GLADSTONE has achieved two immense reforms he is coolly informed that unless something far greater be done Ireland will never be content.

Answer.

The objection begs the question. The very issue is whether equal justice can be said to be done to Ireland while she is refused that control of her own internal affairs without which a distinct civilized community, according to Sir GEORGE GREY, 'is never either prosperous or content.' The Imperial Parliament is to be thanked for two acts of justice : there may possibly be reasons for refusing a third ; but the concession of the two former is no such reason.

As to gratitude, there is really a very general appreciation in Ireland of the labours of the Sessions 1868-69-70, a revived confidence in Government, a renewed belief in the efficiency of constitutional action, a subsidence of revolutionary propaganda : but to expect any exultant popular gratitude would be absurd. The people wish for one thing : they got another ; how expect them to exult?

As to slighting the Imperial Parliament, it was deemed no slight to relieve it of the internal affairs of Canada—why deem it a slight to relieve it of the internal affairs of Ireland ?

As to Mr. GLADSTONE, he is remarkable beyond any statesman of his age for openness to receive impressions, readiness to reconsider opinions, and power of appreciating and assimilating adverse views. How noble for him to complete his great work of justice and reconciliation! It may be that the Federal view is not so unfamiliar to his mind as his more recent utterances would indicate. In his memorable speech on the Address in 1866 he expressed himself as follows. The words were spoken without any reference to the Federal proposal, but they indicate an appreciation of the facts which appear to justify it. 'For my own part, I will only say that I consider we are a united people, with a common government, with a complete political incorporation. But we are also a United Kingdom, made up of three nations, welded politically into one, but necessarily, and in fact, with many distinctions of law, of usage, of character, of history, and of religion. In circumstances such as these there are common questions, which must be administered upon principles common to the whole Empire—all those questions in which the interests of the whole overbear and swallow up the interests of the parts. . . . But there are many other questions with regard to which in England, Scotland, and Ireland, that interest which is especially English, Scotch, or Irish predominates over that which is common, and with regard to the questions falling within this category we ought to apply to Ireland the same principles on which we act in the two other countries, and legislate for them according to the views of the majority of the people of that country.'*

Objection XV.

The Federal system is, after all, a clumsy and antiquated one. It is suited only to communities in the less advanced stages of social progress. The movement towards it is reactionary. The tendency of the age is towards centralization. Why ask us to go back while all the world is going forward?

Answer.

This objection has been put forward so often that its mere repetition forces it on the mind. But, I find no warrant for it in principle or in fact. So far from the system being clumsy, Mr. FREEMAN pronounces it

---

* Hansard, Part I., 1866. See also Mr. CASHEL HOEY's eloquent and trenchant pamphlet, *Why is Ireland Irreconcilable?* (London : Burns, Oates & Co.)

'the most finished and artificial production of political ingenuity,'* and Mr. MILL teaches that where the conditions for Federal union exist 'their multiplication is always a benefit to the world.'† So far from being reactionary, we have seen that Mr. LAING holds it to be 'that towards which civilised and educated society is naturally tending.'‡ Latterly, indeed, there has been a tendency towards centralization ; but the best thinkers in all countries appear to concur with the best practical statesmen in deeming this latter tendency one not to be encouraged, but to be resisted. Whatever may be said of the distinguished President of the Poor Law Board, he cannot be truly set down as a reactionary politician : yet, addressing his constituents the other day at Halifax, he is reported to have reprobated this latter tendency, and declared himself in favour of 'summoning into life the local government of the country which modern times and modern civilization have allowed to fall into decay,' and of 'the

---

* *Hist. Fed. Gov.*, p. 3.   † *Rep. Gov.*, p. 128.
‡ Notes, &c. p. 27.

promotion of the habits, faculty, and practice of local self-government, in which all intelligent and thinking men of all parties are agreed to believe.' Mr. STANSFELD spoke without reference to Ireland or to the Federal system ; but his testimony is the more valuable for being incidental and involuntary. However, it needs no marshalling of authorities to show that the system under which the United States, Switzerland, Sweden, and Norway flourish, and which has been lately adopted in Australia, Canada, the Austro-Hungarian Empire and the new Germanic Empire, cannot be justly characterised as antiquated or reactionary.

Objection XVI.

In the preceding pages much importance has been rightly attached to the teachings of Mr. MILL and Mr. FREEMAN. Now, both these authorities have declared against the system for which this work is a plea. Mr. MILL expressly declares that ' any form of Federal union between Great Britain and Ireland would be unsatisfactory while it lasted, and would end either in total conquest or in complete separation,'* and that the conditions of fitness which he lays down for successful Federation do not exist in Ireland.† Mr. Freeman expressly says, ' that no one could wish to cut up our United Kingdom into a Federation, to invest English counties with the rights of American states, or even to restore Scotland and Ireland to the quasi-federal positions which they held before their respective unions,'‡ and that Federalism is in its place when it appears in the form of closer union between elements which were distinct, not when it divides members which have hitherto been more closely united.§

Answer.

These eminent authorities appear to be averse to the proposal under discussion. Their opinions are of great weight. It would have been inexcusably uncandid not to have stated these adverse opinions. It would be extremely unwise not to consider them. But no two au-

---

* *England and Ireland*, p. 35.
† *Representative Govt.*, p. 124.   ‡ *Hist. Fed. Gov.*, p. 90.
§ Ibid. p. 108.

thorities, however eminent, can be considered as final on such a question. If I mistake not, they would be the first to disclaim a pretension to set aside by their mere *dicta* the wishes and claims of a great community, cherished through long ages, and existing now in unabated vigour. Besides, when these *dicta* were pronounced the issue was not formally raised. Even the greatest judicial authorities are to be relied on, not for their incidental utterances, but for their final judgments on subjects regularly brought to issue. If it were not presumptuous to enter into disputation with Mr. MILL, one might, I think, show that the conditions of fitness for Federal government which he lays down are amply fulfilled by the circumstances of the case. Moreover, against the *dicta* above quoted are to be set Mr. MILL's own *dictum* that ' every civilised country is entitled to settle its internal affairs in its own way, and no other country ought to interfere with its discretion ; because one country, even with the best intentions, has no chance of understanding the internal affairs of another,'*

* Letter on the Westminster Election, April 17, 1865.

and his admission that 'Irishmen are sufficiently numerous to constitute a respectable
nationality by themselves.'* As to Mr. FREE-
MAN's observation, though it indicates a tendency, it does not pronounce any judgment
on the case in hand. It is not now proposed
to restore Ireland to the quasi-federal position
she held before the Union ; no one dreams of
giving English counties the rights of American
states ; and the special justification pleaded
for the present proposal is, that, by a fit adjustment of legislative and administrative powers,
it will tend to form a better understanding,
and therefore a closer union, between elements
which have always been distinct, and which
for centuries have been antagonistic. But if
when the question is fairly raised these great
authorities formally pronounce against the proposal under discussion, one can only regret the
circumstance, avail of it to take precautions
against possible contingencies, and console
oneself with the belief that a case must be very
strong indeed which can be proved by the ad-
missions of even its most eminent adversaries.

* *Rep. Gov.*, p. 123.

Objection XVII.

The progress of events has so weakened royal authority that, whatever may have been the case in O'CONNELL's time, it would be utterly unsafe now to let the connection between the two countries depend on ' the golden link of the Crown.' Loyalty to the Crown has now no practical meaning except acquiescence in the sovereignty of the House of Commons.

Answer.

The distinction between the present proposal and that of O'CONNELL is precisely this : that, whereas O'CONNELL's did, the present proposal does not, allow the connection between the two countries to depend on ' the golden link of the Crown.'   Under the arrangement now under discussion all the material securities for connection will, as we have seen, remain untouched, and they will be enhanced by moral securities which do not exist now, and can never exist under an arrangement with which no civilised community could be, or ought to be, content.   The sovereignty of

the Imperial House of Commons for every
Imperial purpose will continue absolutely un-
impaired, and it will be strengthened by being
relieved from details of Irish domestic arrangements which really do not belong to it, and
which have been only quite recently imposed
upon it.

Objection XVIII.

Under the proposed arrangement the Imperial Parliament would be everything, the
Irish Parliament almost nothing. The greater
assembly would quite overshadow and domi-
nate the lesser one, leaving it neither real
authority nor real dignity. Irish aristocracy
would still seek the more splendid capital;
Irish intellect would still seek the more splendid arena. The Federal scheme may, indeed,
be a compromise more acceptable to England;
but the simple restoration of the Parliament
of '82 is the only thing worth having for
Ireland.

Answer.

I know that this view is shared by some
Irishmen of eminent services and position,

and I differ from them with reluctance and with respect.

In one point, at least, it appears to me to involve an error, namely in the supposition that under the Federal system there is any subordination whatever of the State legislature to the Imperial one. There is no such subordination, direct or indirect, explicit or virtual. Each is supreme in its own sphere. 'The State administration, within its own range, is carried on as freely as if there were no such thing as a Union; the Federal administration, within its own range, is carried on as freely as if there were no such thing as a separate state.'*

It appears to me equally erroneous to suppose that the sphere of the Irish State legislation would be a narrow or unimportant one. We have seen the range of subjects in which, according to Federal principles, it would be supreme.† It would, in fact, possess the administration of all the affairs of the Irish community, excepting only its share of im-

* Freeman, *Hist. Fed. Gov. Con.*, p. 11. Mill, *Rep. Gov.*, p. 125. *Federalist*, No. 9.

† See ante, p. 13.

perial, foreign, or colonial transactions. As a matter of comparison, its sphere would be far the more important to Ireland and to every Irishman than that of Imperial Parliament. I submit that it is not likely that Irishmen of real mark would consider it more honourable to give an occasional vote on a question of foreign policy or colonial administration than to take part in the legislature and administration which would have the exclusive, independent, and sovereign control of the internal affairs of their own country. Even Lord LANSDOWNE admitted that under the Federal arrangement the Irish Parliament would be likely to include 'the best men in the country.'*

Again, whatever special advantage might accrue from the adoption of the arrangement of '82 it would have this disadvantage, that it would reduce Ireland to the position of a colony. Under it, as Mr. BUTT shows,† Ireland had no voice in the making of peace or war, no share in the management of the Colonies, no control over the army or navy, no part in international affairs; and even

* Speech at Kenmare, September 1871.   † *Federalism*, p. 37.

Irish bills had to be submitted to the English
Privy Council and certified under the Great
Seal of England before they became law.
Under the true Federal system Ireland would
possess a full proportionate share of influence
in questions of peace and war, and in all international, colonial, military, and naval
affairs ; and no English Minister or Privy
Council would have the slightest jurisdiction
over her internal affairs. Why should Irishmen prefer the less independent, less dignified,
and less influential position ?

Again, I submit that in effecting a new
settlement of the relations between the two
countries, it is better to select a perfect than
an imperfect type. The arrangement of '82
was, as Lord BROUGHAM says, only an 'imperfect' or 'improper' federation. Ireland's
position, as Mr. FREEMAN says, was not really
Federal, but only 'quasi-Federal;' the arrangement belonged to the class of 'lax confede-
racies' of which the late German BUND was
a conspicuous, but not encouraging, example.
I submit that it would now be better to revert
to the true Federal type, so well settled by

great statesmen, so well studied by political philosophers, so well tested by long and varied experience. It is nearly always safer to deal with settled systems and to tread beaten ways than to venture on new and almost untried combinations. Under the former all educated men know what they are about and see only what they foresaw ; under the latter all would be experimental, tentative, thick set with perilous contingencies. ' *Via trita, via tuta.*'

Again : the imperfect dualism of '82 is subject to the objection that, like all imperfect things, it is apt to get out of order. It nearly always ends either in separation or centralization. The Federal system is almost the only one which, as a matter of fact, has enabled communities to pull together harmoniously while preserving for each the control of its domestic affairs.

Lastly : the project of imperfect dualism is so fraught with danger of separation that its concession by England may fairly be set down as amongst those things which are politically impossible. Great Britain will never consent to separation or to anything leading to it ; and the most influential Irishmen of all classes share the English belief that it is best for both Islands to ' pull together.' On the other hand it is hoped that when the matter comes to be understood, few Englishmen will be found so selfish as to object to Irishmen managing their own internal affairs if it can be shown that such management is compatible with the unity and integrity of the Empire ; and it is hoped that few Irishmen, however much and however rightly they may object to separation, will be found so mean-spirited as to declare themselves incompetent to transact their own special business, under an old well-tried and well-settled political system which has served similar purposes for other communities time out of mind, and under which some of the greatest of existing communities now flourish.

For these reasons I submit that the objection under consideration cannot be relied upon as an argument against the present proposal, and I am strengthened in this belief by the fact that Mr. O'Neill Daunt and other eminent gentlemen who prefer the arrangement of '82 have waived their preference and given the most valuable support to the present proposal as the nearest practicable approximation to their views.

Objection XIX.

How reconcile the co-ordinate jurisdictions of the two legislations ? How define their limits ? How arbitrate on their disputes ?

Answer.

Some writers put these questions as if they were unheard of novelties and as if their solution were impossible. But it is scarcely necessary to remind well-informed men that they only indicate one of the problems with which the Federal system is most familiar, and which it has satisfactorily solved under the most varying circumstances and in the most different times. I have anticipated the question and indicated the solution at p. 15.*

Objection XX.

How is the Imperial Parliament to levy taxes in Ireland for Imperial purposes ?

* See also Mill, *Rep. Gov.*, p. 126.

Answer.

This is also one of the oldest, commonest, and best-settled problems which arise out of the Federal system. At first it was effected, both in America and Switzerland, by means of requisitions addressed to the State legislatures by the Imperial Congress. But this arrangement was not found to work. Such requisitions could only be carried into effect through orders issued by the local governments to officers appointed by them under the responsibility of their own Courts of Justice, and thus were often neglected or but grudgingly obeyed. In America this error was happily perceived in the lifetime of the great statesmen who founded the Republic and was wisely rectified by them.* In Switzerland the same rectification took place at a later period. The contrary plan is now the settled practice of Federal States, and is deemed by all politico-philosophic authorities essential to the well-working of the system.† Under this plan the powers and rights of the Imperial Parlia-

---

* See *Federalist*, No. 39. De Tocqueville, i. 268.
† Wheaton, *International Law*, i. 68. Mill, *Rep. Gov.*, 125.

ment for all Imperial purposes would remain exactly as they are now. Within the limits of its attributions it would make laws binding every citizen individually, to be executed by its own officers, and enforced by its own tribunals.* 'The real difference between the two plans,' says Mr. FREEMAN, 'is that one is a good, the other a bad, way of accomplishing the same objects.'† 'The attributes of congress,' says Professor BERNARD, 'are the same under both plans: what was done was to make them real and effective by making them operate directly on the people of the States instead of on the States themselves.' ‡ 'We cannot,' says Mr. BUTT, 'propose with any chance of success a Federal constitution for Ireland without leaving the Imperial Parliament the same powers in this respect as those of Congress.' §

Objection XXI.

How is free trade to be maintained? What is to prevent the Irish Parliament

* Mill, Ibid.   † *Hist. Fed. Gov.*, p. 12.
‡ Lectures on American War, p. 69.   § *Federalism*, p. 53.

from establishing differential duties, and re-adopting the fallacies of protection ?

Answer.

So far as the HOME GOVERNMENT ASSOCIATION is concerned these as well as the other details we have been discussing are perfectly open questions. But the rule and practice of the Federal system are clear. All custom duties and general trade regulations are made and regulated by the Federal Government exclusively.* The objection, therefore, falls to the ground.

Objection XXII.

Ireland had a Parliament of its own. Its working resulted in a bloody insurrection. It was so little prized that the Irish sold it for a few titles and some money. It is absurd to go back to where we left off in the last century and restore an institution which, admittedly, was unsound in principle, which worked badly in practice, which was sold as

* Mill, *Fed. Gov.*, p. 127.

a bauble by one country, and which was abolished as a nuisance by the other.

Answer.

The present proposal is not one for the restoration of the Parliament of '82, but for quite a different thing, namely, a Parliament on the Federal principle. The objection is therefore irrelevant.

For that matter I suppose no one would desire to reconstitute as it was a Parliament most of whose Peerages were given away for English services, more than half of whose Commons were returned as nominees for close boroughs, and inside whose portals no one of the creed of the people could enter. If an institution, so imperfect in principle and so ill-constituted in fact, had worked badly, it would afford no argument whatever against a Federal Parliament right in principle and properly constituted in fact.

But, as it happens, the Parliament of '82 did not work badly. Notwithstanding its defects, it worked well on the whole. Contemporary authorities are nearly unanimous

on this point. In Lord PLUNKET's great speech
of January 1800, he thus describes the progress of Ireland under the Parliament of '82 :
' Her revenues, her trade, her manufactures,
prospered beyond the example of any other
country of her extent. Within these few
years they advanced with a rapidity astonish-
ing even to herself.' Lord PLUNKET's antago-
nist, Lord CLARE, in a pro-union pamphlet
quoted by GRATTAN, admitted that ' there is
not a nation on the habitable globe which
has advanced in cultivation and commerce, in
agriculture and manufactures, with the same
rapidity in the same period.'

A score of similar testimonies might be
quoted to show that even this imperfect system of self-government worked well. How
much better may we hope would be the working of a better system !

As to the transaction by which its existence
was terminated, it is admittedly ' tainted with
fraud.' No principle can be deduced from a
swindle. You might as well argue that a
man should never wear a watch because it
happened that he was once swindled out of
an imperfect old family time-piece.

Finally, it is not accurate to say that the Irish sold their Parliament. As to the Irish people, their voice was against the Union. But the bulk of the people were not represented in the matter at all. It was settled by the nominees of 'rotten boroughs' and their masters — a class not remarkable for purity of political principle in any country. Such people sold themselves, their votes, and their influence at this period as readily in England as they did in Ireland. It would be equally fallacious in either case to found on this corruption an objection to parliamentary institutions, or to the right of a civilised community to the control of its own affairs.

Objection XXIII.

Underlying the argument of the preceding pages, there runs an assumption that the Irish community is in favour of this proposal. Now this assumption is an error. With a few exceptions, the landed aristocracy, the gentry, and the Protestant clergy are against it. The Catholic clergy have not declared for it. The Orangemen have declared against it. The Fenians are

not satisfied with it. Even the HOME GOVERN-
MENT ASSOCIATION itself is not unanimous in
its favour, and is certainly very far from being
unanimous as to the details suggested by Mr.
BUTT, or prescribed by political philosophy as
essential to the right working of the Federal
system. In fact, nobody is in favour of this
proposal except a few agitators in Dublin, the
mobs of a few cities set in motion by these,
some Members of Parliament who want to
keep their seats at all sacrifices, and some
aspiring gentlemen who want to become
Members of Parliament on any terms.

Answer.

I have not in any place assumed that the
Irish community is in favour of this proposal.
What I have assumed is, that the vast majority of Irishmen are in favour of civil liberty
and self-government in *some* form. This is
incontestably true. If there be any one point
about which popular feeling is distinct, un-
varying, enthusiastic, it is this. To a large,
and daily increasing, extent the educated
opinion of cultivated men and the practical

conclusions of men of business coincide on this point with popular feeling. Indeed, public spirit should have sunk very low in any community, nay, individual self-respect should be sadly wanting, if it were otherwise. It is difficult to conceive a civilized community really declaring that it is incompetent to transact its own business, opposing the concession of civil liberty to itself, and demanding its own subjection as a boon.

The reasonable desire for self-government in some form being thus clear, and this proposal being made as a means of legitimately and safely satisfying it, I have considered the proposal on its merits and endeavoured to adduce reasons in favour of its adoption. These reasons may be valid or invalid, but their validity or invalidity in no respect depends on 'count of heads.' They might be of the most perfect validity even though a score of persons had not declared for the proposal; they might be utterly invalid even though everybody concerned had adopted it.

But, as a matter of fact, the principle of the proposal has obtained a more general acceptance in Ireland than any political proposal of the last quarter of a century. It is well known that many of the leading gentry are inclined to it. The clergy, with few exceptions, view it favourably. Most municipalities have adhered to it. The people have hailed it with enthusiasm almost everywhere. The Hon. David Plunket, M.P., tells us it will have, at least, seventy advocates in Parliament after next election. Shrewd, sensible, well-informed non-politicians of all creeds and parties are entertaining it favourably. It has become an ' idea of the day ' and come fairly ' to the front ' for public discussion and parliamentary settlement. If there were a *plebiscite* to-morrow in Ireland it would be adopted by a majority of millions.

Objection XXIV.

What Ireland needs is to be governed from without. The people are too unruly for liberty. They wrest every political privilege for evil ends. They condone assassination and cheer the assassin. They swallow any nonsense if it be only flavoured with sedition. The Bishop of WINCHESTER's prescription indicates the only successful mode of dealing with Irishmen :— 'feed them well, treat them well, and when they do wrong wallop them well.'

Answer.

To the very limited extent to which there is any basis of fact for this objection the fact is to be lamented. So far as any political privilege is perverted, or the fearful crime of assassination deliberately condoned, or any one believed to be an assassin applauded, or nonsense with or without sedition swallowed, it is to be regretted ; the honour of Ireland is by so much tarnished ; the cause of progress and liberty is by so much retarded. But in what country could the objector live that he would not have to lament some such evils ? Not in England certainly, for there the Sheffield assassins were applauded by the populace, ORSINI was patronized, GARIBALDI lionized, POOK acquitted, BRADLAUGH tolerated, and blasphemous sedition again and again cheered by vast assemblages in the great square of the Metropolis. Are Englishmen prepared, on this account, to ask Prince Bismark to administer, (as surely none could so well as he,) the good Bishop's political prescription? If such evils do not disqualify one island for freedom, why are evil tendencies far less developed held to disqualify the other?

Moreover, we must not forget that the very existence of such evils, so far as they do exist, is an argument for civil liberty. To a community, as to a man, subjection is a constant irritant. It sets life ajar, embitters feud, enkindles hate, intensifies passion, diminishes self-respect, and checks the growth of that self-control which can scarcely exist without liberty. You persist in ruling Ireland on a system which Irishmen hate; which (as I submit) common sense, experience, and political philosophy condemn; and then you open your eyes with wonder that everything does not go right. It is the very case of the advocates of reform that under the present system things are pretty certain to go wrong. But remove the irritant, give the country the fair chance which every civilized community requires, and let all abide the result. If history teach any one lesson more emphatically than another, it is the lesson that communities thrive with freedom and deteriorate under subjection.

'A Parliament in Dublin,' wrote the *Spectator* the other day with characteristic acuteness and fairness, ' would put down agrarian murders and conspiracy with an iron hand, compared with which that of the United Parliament is soft as velvet.'

Objection XXV.

A few months ago sensible men of all parties in Ireland were inclining towards the Home Government proposal. But the violence of language and conduct indulged in by some of its supporters has turned the tide of opinion against it. Whatever individual inclinations or judgments may be, self-respecting men cannot identify themselves with unreasoning violence of speech or conduct.

Answer.

Of all objections to the Home Government proposal this is the one most frequently

alleged in private conversation. It shows
how intemperate advocacy may prejudice a
cause. But I submit that it is the most completely illogical and unreasonable of any.
Indeed it has hardly ventured to show itself
in print at all. It may do for after dinner
debate ; but the ' morning's reflection ' is
fatal to it. In the first place every one
admits that so far as the leaders of the movement are concerned their advocacy has been
conducted in the most conciliatory spirit.
Their mode of speech and action have received
generous praise even from their most vehement
adversaries in the English press. In the next
place it must be remembered that if such fasti-
diousness as the objection implies were univer-
sally indulged, political progress would become impracticable. This is a question of politics, not of politeness. Intemperate advocacy
injures any cause ; but the injury is one which
every cause has, more or less, to endure. Lastly :
I trust it is not an ungenerous ' tu quoque '
to remark that, in this controversy at least,
the chief sinners have not been amongst the
popular ranks. It is not from the advocates

of the proposal have proceeded threats that proceedings which are at least constitutional must be encountered by violence, and that the aspiration towards freedom, which is at least natural, must be extinguished 'in blood.'

Objection XXV.

One of the ablest of English periodicals suggests the objection that the proposed system would give Irishmen the Government not only of Ireland but of England.

Answer.

This is a misconception of the Federal system and of the Home Government proposal. On the Federal plan Irish members would have nothing whatever to do with the internal affairs of England or Scotland, and would have only a proportionate and co-ordinate share in imperial, colonial, and foreign affairs.

Objection XXVI.

Another great organ of public opinion

makes the contrary objection that a Federal
plan would reduce Ireland to the position of
a colony.

Answer.

This objection is clearly an oversight.
On the Federal plan the relations of Great
Britain and Ireland would be those of complete equality. Each would manage separately the affairs which concern itself only.
Both would manage together the affairs which
concern both. Surely Massachusetts does not
stand in the relation of a colony to the
American Union ; or Berne to Switzerland ;
or Norway to Sweden ; or Hungary to Austria ; or Bavaria to Germany.

Objection XXVII.

A political project to which even an advocate can state twenty-six plausible objections
must, to say the least, be an objectionable
proposal.

Answer.

Not at all. Ten times as many plausible

objections might be raised to any political institution or arrangement whatsoever; nay, would certainly be raised, if, like the present, it were a proposal merely. It is easy enough to overlook objections, or to pretend to mis-understand them, or not to take the trouble to appreciate them, or so to state them that they almost answer themselves, or to answer them captiously or disingenuously, or with slap-dash generalisations. But no con-clusion is worth much which is thus arrived at. I trust my reader will be better pleased that, having first clearly defined my own views, I have endeavoured to study and ap-preciate the views of every adversary, to state them as spiritedly and as fairly as I could, and to give to them the full, patient, and cautious consideration which every legitimate objection deserves.

CHAPTER VI.

Conclusion.

WE have now gone over the whole ground of the present controversy. I have endeavoured to state the proposal in principle and to elucidate it in detail, to show that it is consistent with common sense, with political philosophy and with the results of the world's experience, to explain the practical advantages which are expected from it, and to consider every legitimate objection to it. I have tried to do this with the severe impartiality of a philosophic student and the practical caution of one who has some stake in the country. I trust I have written no word, as I am certain that I have entertained no thought, unkind to any one concerned, or unjust to any section of the inhabitants of these realms. I hope I may lead some persons to the conclusion at which, on a review of the whole matter, and a balance of all considerations, I have myself most sincerely arrived : the conclusion, namely, that the re-adjustment of the relations between Great Britain and Ireland on the Federal plan would really be advantageous to both Islands. And I respectfully submit these pages as my contribution to a momentous controversy, commenced long ages ago, continued in various ways through all changes of fortune, and now, I hope, to be satisfactorily settled at last : a controversy in which, however it be settled, are involved the peace of my own declining years, the prospects of my children, the security of whatever my industry has accumulated, the welfare of fellow-countrymen from every section of whom I have received life-long favours, the safety of England, to whom, with all her faults, every educated man is a debtor, and the prosperity of Ireland, which all her sons should, each in his measure and according to his light, sincerely endeavour to promote.

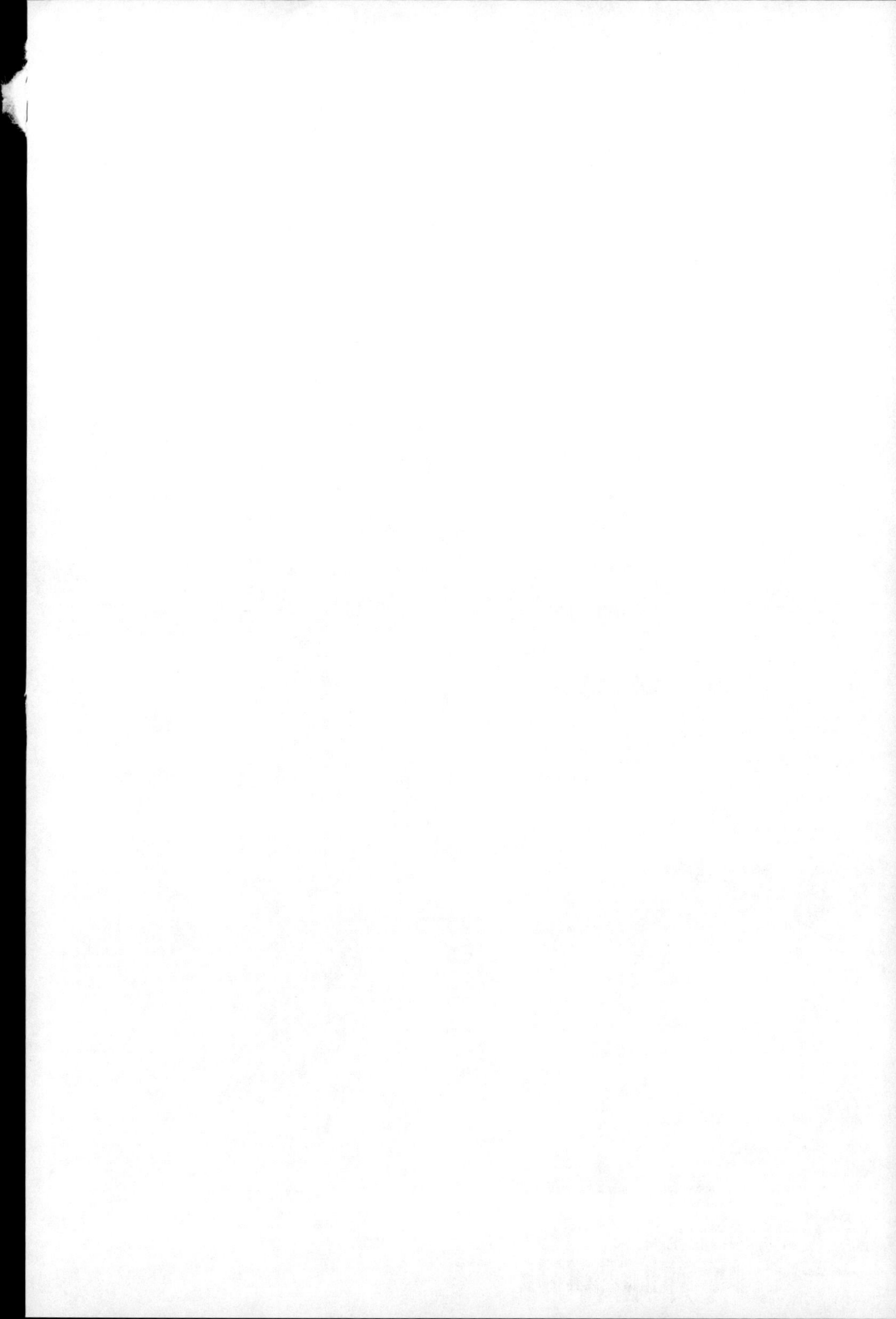

www.ingramcontent.com/pod-product-compliance
Lightning Source LLC
Chambersburg PA
CBHW030828270326
41928CB00007B/947